ENCYCLOPEDIA

OF

PHYSICAL BITCOINS

AND

CRYPTO-CURRENCIES

ELIAS AHONEN

FOREWORD BY
MATTHEW J. RIPPON PHD

EDITED BY
HOWARD KESSELMAN

ENCYCLOPEDIA
OF
PHYSICAL BITCOINS
AND
CRYPTO-CURRENCIES

FIRST EDITION

2016

Contact: **author@coinfirm.org**

Ordering Information:
Paperback and/or digital copies may occasionally be purchased directly from the author, or at any time from approved distributors.
Discounts are available on quantity purchases.

To place an order for any quantity of books, contact the author at the email address above.

Ahonen, Elias.
Encyclopedia of Physical Bitcoins and Crypto-Currencies / Elias Ahonen

ISBN 978-0-9950899-0-7

1. ANTIQUES & COLLECTIBLES — Coins, Currency & Medals. 2. BUSINESS & ECONOMICS — Money & Monetary Policy. 3. COMPUTERS — Information Technology.
ANT011000
BUS045000
COM032000

Thema Subjects: Antiques & collectables; Business studies: general; Encyclopaedias & reference works; Reference works; General encyclopaedias; Flags, emblems, symbols, logos; Interdisciplinary studies; Inventions & inventors; Collecting coins, banknotes, medals, seals (numismatics); Antiques & collectables: gold, silver & other metals (other than jewellery); Media studies: Internet, digital media & society; Popular culture; Material culture; Political control & freedoms

First Edition

These coins are the lasting physical evidence
Of the long process of technological and social progress
Which will bring forth a new understanding of value
With all its unknown consequences

This book is dedicated to the physical manifestation
Of a trail-blazing culture of
Innovators, ideologues, entrepreneurs, and artists
Who will one day cause the world to move

Table of Contents

About the Authors

Elias Ahonen

At the time of writing, Elias is completing the last year of his Honors Bachelor in Political Science at Wilfrid Laurier University in Waterloo, Ontario, Canada. In 2014 he published a free eBook guide to Casascius physical bitcoins, which was well received and turned into this much larger project in part due to popular demand. Having been interested in Bitcoin since early 2013, he has built a varied collection of physical crypto-currency. In addition to its technological merits, he sees digital currency as a fascinating case study in economics, public opinion, regulation, the culture that has formed around it, and the differing ways in which it is interpreted by people of various ideological viewpoints (many of which are reflected in the physical coins themselves). His other interests include travel, photography, philosophy, entrepreneurship, and futurology.

Matthew J. Rippon PhD

Matthew earned his BSc in International History in 2001 from the London School of Economics and Political Science. In 2008, he was awarded an MSc in Globalisation and Development at Queen Mary, University of London. His PhD, at the same institution, studied the intellectual property of geographically-specific food names. Matthew's current interests include crypto-currency, financial technology, libertarianism, black and white photography, and Russian literature. He became interested in Bitcoin in early 2012 and attended the London Bitcoin conference in September of that year. Matthew is currently writing a paper about innovators and entrepreneurs in the Bitcoin economy. In January 2016, he was granted Certified Bitcoin Professional (CBP) status by the Crypto-Currency Certification Consortium (C4).

Howard Kesselman

Howard (aka. Bitcointalk.org user 'bithalo') is an 'avid' collector of physical crypto-currencies, with a wide interest in coins, paper wallets, and cards. While he does not focus on collecting 'rounds' that have no capability of storing crypto-currency, he is interested in pre-funded, empty, and DIY coins. The diverse collection, which he has been expanding since January 2014, contains over 200 different physical wallets by more than 50 manufacturers. He earned his Master of Science in Finance (MSF) degree at Florida International University and has over 20 years experience in finance and technology. Currently, he is an IT Consulting Manager and lives in Lake Worth, Florida, USA.

Acknowledgments

In this non-exhaustive list, I would like to thank the following:

David Bailey
For proofreading and analyzing his HardBTC store inventory to help with my research.

Matt Moss
For creating the useful Uberbills coin tracker.

Mike Caldwell
For taking the time to discuss his experiences.

Everyone who shared their specialized knowledge with Matthew and myself, including but not limited to Scott Barnett, Took Groth, 'JJC', Morris La Mantia, and a large number of manufacturers.

Everyone who shared their photos with me, allowing this guide to represent the coins in the best way possible.

Manufacturers that provided me with samples of their coins.

Everyone who pre-ordered this book, including:

Adrian Forbes
Alemanno Antonio
Andrew J. Schaffer
Chris Crawford
C. Mitchell
Danny Uvdmnte
D. Lauda
Dexter Barnett
E. M. Jones
El Conde de Granada
Hans G
J. Dozerz John Sacco
Jon Allen
Keeth Beharrell
Kolten Wilson
Michail Wilson
Orlando M. García
Patrick van der Kruis
Pawel Karbowski
P. Cyclops
Raimon Poves
Reed Taylor
Scott Barnett
Took Groth

Glossary

Alt-currency / Alt-coin: One of over 500 crypto-currencies inspired by Bitcoin. Many use technologies that are viewed by proponents as improvements to Bitcoin.

ANACS: The oldest coin grading service in America, which has become the most popular service for grading physical crypto-currencies in coin-form.

Balance: The amount of BTC or alt-currency in an address.

Bitcent: A common name for 1/100th (0.01) of a Bitcoin.

Bitcoin: The first and most widely used decentralized crypto-currency.

Bitcointalk.org: A popular internet discussion forum focusing on Bitcoin, including sub-forums for technical support, mining, development and economics. Similar forums exist for many alt-currencies.

Blockchain: The transaction database shared by all nodes participating in a system based on the Bitcoin protocol. A full copy of a currency's blockchain contains every transaction ever executed in the currency.

Buyer-Funded: A balance has been added to the coin by the buyer before shipment.

Certificate: A document issued by the manufacturer pertaining to a particular coin, usually to guarantee authenticity. They sometimes include the public key and serial number.

Coin: Conventionally, a piece of metal that is 'legal tender' issued by a government. In the crypto-coin context, it refers to a piece of metal with the intended function of containing a balance.

Cold Storage: Crypto-currency stored 'offline' and as such not quick to access and theoretically impossible to hack. Methods include USB sticks, offline hard-drives, paper-wallets, or physical coins.

Denomination: The amount of crypto-currency displayed on the coin, irrespective of funding. When no specific number is displayed, the currency code is used to indicate the coin's theme.

FinCEN: The Financial Crimes Enforcement Network (FinCEN) is a bureau of the United States Department of the Treasury that collects and analyzes information about financial transactions in order to combat domestic and international money laundering, terrorist financing, and other financial crimes.

Funded / Loaded: The state of an address (specifically an address pertaining to a coin) having a balance.

Grade: The numismatic grade given to a physical coin by a service such as ANACS.

Litecoin: One of the first crypto-currencies, inspired by Bitcoin. As of writing it is the 2nd most popular crypto-currency.

Microbit / μBTC: A common name for 1/1,000,000th (0.000001) of a Bitcoin.

Millibit / mBTC: A common name for 1/1,000th (0.001) of a Bitcoin.

Mining: The process of adding transaction records to Bitcoin's public ledger of past transactions, known as the blockchain.

Mintage: The number of coins known or believed to have been created.

Physical Crypto-currency: A fluid definition of crypto-currency in a 'physical form' such as coins, bars, cards, or even paper wallets. This guide focuses exclusively on the 'coin' (and 'bar') form.

Plate / Pl.: The state of a coin being thinly covered (plated) by a metal other than that of which the coin is composed of. This is often done for aesthetics or durability.

Pre-Funded: A balance has been added to a coin by the manufacturer before shipment.

Private Key Pit: A recess stamped onto the back of physical crypto-currency in order to allow a piece of paper containing the private key to rest securely under the hologram.

Private Key: The 'password' to the BTC contained in any address (Public Key). This can be used to withdraw the balance of its address at any time.

Public Key: The 'address' in which any amount of Bitcoin is/can be contained. The amount of BTC contained is visible publicly by looking up the address, and anyone can add BTC to the address.

QR Code: A 'Quick Response Code' which can be scanned by a smartphone. In the physical crypto-currency context this can be used to either check the balance of a coin (Public Key) or 'sweep' the balance of an address to another address (Private Key). It is quick compared to entering a long string of characters.

Round: Traditionally, a piece of metal mimicking currency in design but not issued by any government or having a legal tender value. In the crypto-coin context, it refers to pieces of metal with a crypto-currency 'theme' but which are not designed to actually hold a balance.

Satoshi: The name for the smallest possible unit of Bitcoin which is 1/100,000,000th (0.00000001) BTC. Originally, the word refers to the creator of Bitcoin.

Serial Number / Serialization: Numbers engraved or otherwise noted on the coin (or on a certificate) indicating a specific number assigned to a coin. These generally start from 1 and continue onwards.

Sticker / Hologram: a sticker affixed or intended to be affixed to a coin, with the purpose of securing a private key. Normally, they have holographic elements.

Unfunded: A coin with a working address is shipped to the buyer without a balance.

Introduction

I bought my first physical Bitcoins in April 2013, when I purchased three 1 BTC Casascius coins online due to a combination of curiosity and the desire to hold some of my BTC in physical form as to avoid loss. At that time, I was fairly well acquainted with bitcoin and had acquired some earlier in the year after learning about the digital currency. These first coins turned into additional acquisitions, as I learned more about Casascius physical Bitcoins which were the only coin-like physical crypto-currency products available at the time. As my interest grew and the value of BTC increased, I began turning a small profit and further expanding my collection by buying, selling, and trading the coins online.

One day in June 2014 while reading *The 4-Hour Work Week* by Timothy Ferriss, I became inspired to take on some interesting project that I was well placed to execute. Within moments, I came to realize that nobody had yet written about physical crypto-currency in an extensive and organized fashion, and that I was in a perfect place to do so due to my knowledge base and free time. I immediately decided that I would write a book categorizing all Casascius physical Bitcoins, giving collectors a reliable source of information. I began my work that day, and managed to complete the 31 page *The CoinFIRM Casascius Guide v1* before my free 30 day trial of Adobe InDesign ran out. Numerous enthusiasts provided assistance with this project, including Charlie Shrem, the founder of BitInstant which was one of the first bitcoin exchanges, who assisted in matters of general guidance. Andrew Dobbins started a virtual 'Bitcoin Museum' collecting various Bitcoin memorabilia, and helped the project with photos and data about various specs. Matt Moss runs a 'coin analyzer' which tracks the public addresses of thousands of physical crypto-currencies, and provided me with invaluable data regarding redeemed and funded coins. I also received a sponsorship from David Bailey who runs HardBTC, an online store selling physical crypto-currencies. The website from which the eBook can be freely downloaded has been visited over 25,000 times to date, but the actual readership of the guide is difficult to estimate as the PDF has been often circulated online as a stand-alone document.

As I was writing my initial guide, I received queries asking if I would be focusing exclusively on Casascius coins. These requests inspired me to explore the possibility of expanding the project. As I published the Casascius Guide in July 2014, I announced my next project on the last page of the guide:

> COMING SOON:
> *The Comprehensive CoinFIRM Guide to Physical Bitcoins*
> (or something like that) Expect over 120 pages categorizing every
> crypto-themed coin, round, and bar ever made along with manufacturer
> profiles, lots of interesting info, and much MORE!

Fast forward 20 months to March 2016: the book is finally ready for publication.

My original intention was to complete the book by January 2015. I planned to release the work for free, covering my costs by putting small banner ads or occasional larger ads on the majority of pages. In practice, this was to work by individual manufacturers sponsoring the pages on which their coins appeared. Due to the rapidly increasing selection of physical crypto-currencies on the market, the scope of the book expanded much beyond the originally intended 120 pages. This expansion, along with competing personal priorities and the unexpected difficulties that occur when trying to publish a book, led to a multitude of delays. After the January 2015 completion was not achieved, the timeline was pushed to April 2015, followed by July 2015, December 2015, January 2016, and finally to April 2016.

In April 2015, I announced pre-orders of a limited edition paperback version of the otherwise at the time free (at the time) eBook. I also created a crowd-funder, which initially raised over 1000 USD but failed due to errors I made in the set-up phase that prescribed a slightly higher 'minimum amount' than that which was raised. As the crowd-funding site was based in the UK and therefore received most funding in GBP, I used the same currency to set the base price of the paperback even though I am based in Canada.

In June 2015, I was contacted by Matthew Rippon who wanted to interview me about physical crypto-currencies as part of an article about Bitcoin for *The International Journal of Entrepreneurship and Innovation*. Being very impressed with his research, I had several discussions about physical crypto-currencies with him and directed him to various individuals of interest to expand his research. After the exchange of dozens of emails over a four week period, I asked him to collaborate with me on this book.

With over 300 back-and-forth emails, weekly discussions, and numerous interviews with both manufacturers and collectors, Matthew's contribution has been huge. Being an academic, he has transformed the book from a simple catalogue of coins into a semi-academic work that relays a near complete understanding of physical crypto-currencies to the intelligent layperson who is otherwise uninformed about the subject matter.

In July 2015, I decided to forego the original plan of releasing a free eBook. By doing this, I was better able to focus on creating quality content as opposed to putting my energies into selling ad space. This decision was made in response to feedback I received from several potential buyers, who felt that the ads took away from the professionalism of the work and did not reflect well on the hobby of collecting physical crypto-currencies as a whole. I agreed with the sentiment, saying that "this is a professional, specialized publication" as opposed to a more casual magazine-like publication that commonly displays such ads.

Howard Kesselman was originally contacted by Matthew who arranged an interview with him to gain knowledge from an established collector. He displayed great enthusiasm in the project and unreservedly offered his assistance. Howard has proved extremely helpful, going to great lengths checking and adding to the database from which all of the coin specs are derived. In addition, he has taken many photos of his own extensive collection to ensure quality images throughout the *Encyclopedia*. Since November 2015, he has been working directly with Matthew and myself.

As I have learned in the months leading up to publication, writing a book like this is no small task. Matthew, Howard, and I have all expressed amazement at the amount of work that has actually been put in. I am the first to admit that had I suspected the process to be as complex as it has been, it is unlikely I would have began in the first place. One problem that came to light in the late stage of completion was that of proportion and print quality. As I discovered, a computer monitor displays an image perfectly at 72 PPI (pixels per inch), whereas a printed photo requires 300 PPI. This meant that while my book which was configured in 100 PPI looked great when viewed on a monitor, it did not quite meet the quality standards of professional printing. To fix this, I hired a freelancer who had to individually copy, paste, and enlarge each element of the book; a task which took over two weeks. One interesting thing that has been continually encountered are the surprisingly large number of variations between standard spellings and grammatical nuances between UK, US, and Canadian English. Quite humorously, having a PhD edit hundreds of pages of one's writing is a rather humbling process, and I have discovered many opportunities to improve my writing and change some habits when it comes to certain uses of grammar and punctuation. Overall, writing this *Encyclopedia* with a highly motivated and competent team has been an incredibly rewarding experience full of learning and personal development.

Throughout the book, the best available photos and the most reliable sources of information have been used for the purpose of accurately recording the physical crypto-currency phenomenon for perpetuity. Due to the nature of the subject matter including rarity, unavailability, and expense, it is not practical to personally produce quality photos of all subjects in a standardized fashion. As such, the quality and style of photos vary as they have been taken by a number of individuals and businesses with varying equipment and ability. All written content has been produced by the authors and/or editor unless where cited otherwise.

The majority of photos have either been taken by the authors/editor, or direct permission has been granted by the original photographer. A significant subset of photos and graphics such as logos have been taken or created by the coin manufacturers for promotional and/

or informational purposes and posted publicly to the Internet. Some photos have been posted publicly on the Internet by anonymous or pseudo-anonymous individuals for the purpose of educating viewers about the coins. In this environment, the original photographer cannot always be reliably identified or contacted. All photos in this *Encyclopedia* are meant for the purposes of commentary and scholarship, and are ultimately used under the Fair Use doctrine of copyright law which allows limited use of copyrighted material without attribution or permission from the rights holders for such purposes.

In a similar vein, it should be remembered that information regarding some of the coins contained in this book can be very difficult to come by and/or verify. As such, all information presented, specifically in the spec boxes, are accurate to the best understanding of the authors/editor. Some information is missing on a number of coins. While the *Encyclopedia* documents all notable physical crypto-currencies released, a few other varieties are known to exist, and have been intentionally left out due to the information regarding them being so insubstantial that devoting a page to such a coin would reflect badly on the work as a whole. Adding them all would have resulted in many pages with very low quality images (or no images at all) with few if any specs available, and nothing more than a sentence or two of intelligent commentary on an otherwise blank entry. I am confident that a good balance has been struck between comprehensiveness and overall quality.

For readers who are anything less then experts in the subject matter, I highly recommend the following reading order. After reading the Foreword, skip directly to the *Casascius* section on pages 79-115, followed by the *Lealana* section on pages 185-197.

While I certainly owe the greatest gratitude to Matthew and Howard for their expert contributions, I wish to extend a further message of thanks to the wider community of physical crypto-currency collectors and manufacturers. It is your collective appreciation for my work that has inspired me to create this book. Furthermore, it is the numerous messages of excitement, unreserved offers of help, and anticipation for the completed work, even after over a year of delays and changes, that have kept my focus on the goal. In addition to this, I have been honored by the trust and support given to me by everyone who has pre-ordered this book.

To all those who share an interest in physical crypto-currencies, your inspiration and enthusiasm is the very reason for its existence. This book belongs to you.

Elias Ahonen
March 2016

Foreword to Encyclopedia of Physical Bitcoins and Crypto-Currencies

Introduction

Bitcoin is a unique monetary system which provides a viable digital alternative to national currencies like the dollar, euro, pound, renminbi, and yen. It is designed by an anonymous programmer that called himself Satoshi Nakamoto[1] who, on 1 November 2008, released a white paper entitled *Bitcoin: A Peer-to-Peer Electronic Cash System.*[2] Bitcoin is novel because currency – bitcoin[3] – is generated by mining nodes that solve a demanding mathematical challenge known as a 'proof-of-work'.[4] Nakamoto designed Bitcoin to be a self-regulating economic system in which participants are not required to trust each other. Rather, nodes that comprise the peer-to-peer network constantly check to ensure that participants act honestly.[5]

Most people in the West have heard of Bitcoin but their understanding is, at best, superficial and, at worst, hostile. Unfortunately, for many, the word 'Bitcoin' conjurers up unpalatable images of malevolent drug dealers selling narcotics on so-called 'dark markets' like the Silk Road.[6] Others might regard Bitcoin as unstable due to the price volatility of November 2013 when one bitcoin was worth over 1,100 USD.[7] Yet another group may inarticulately claim that Bitcoin is a 'Ponzi' or 'pyramid' scheme.[8] Those who have taught themselves about Bitcoin, work in the crypto-currency industry, use bitcoin to buy goods and services, or retain the currency as a store of value constitute a fraction of the populace.

Bitcoin has many attractive features. It is anti-inflationary as a maximum of 21 million coins will be mined, divisible as each BTC (the unit of currency) can be segregated into 100,000,000 pieces, transferable as it is digital, almost free due to minimal transaction fees, decentralized with no need for banks, universal so that anyone can buy and sell bitcoin, and pseudo-anonymous although transactions are recorded on the public blockchain.

In the seven years since the 'genesis block' was mined in January 2009, entrepreneurs have created a vast array of new industries which include exchanges, mining pools, bitcoin ATM's, hardware wallets, and Bitcoin 2.0 companies.[9] One of the most appealing yet overlooked innovations is physical Bitcoin.[10] This *Encyclopedia* is the first work to professionally catalogue physical Bitcoin and hence seeks to redress the dearth of research into this important subject.[11]

This Introduction contextualizes the information provided in the body of the *Encyclopedia*. It defines physical Bitcoin, and, through the notion of 'material culture', explores their physical attributes, economic value, symbolic elements, ideological components, social form, trust requirements, and technical facets. It develops a typology of producers, seeks to understand how the market values coins (using 'value' in its broadest sense), determines how manufacturers distinguish their coins from those of their fellow producers, articulates the regulatory environment, and discusses the attitudes and beliefs of collectors based on information gathered from several telephone interviews. I am most grateful to my respondents for their time and testimony. Finally, the Introduction details the structure of the *Encyclopedia* and explains the data given for each manufacturer and coin.

Physical Bitcoin represents a new way to understand money. It takes the image of national currency coins – their materials, denomination, images, text, and security features – and either adds digital value (funded coins) or depicts a representation of that digital value (unfunded coins). Participants in the physical Bitcoin community emphasize the coins' digital features but, perhaps paradoxically, display the result in 'conventional' coin format.

Funded physical Bitcoin are metal coins which contain the prefix of a public address and a private key.[12] The public address is openly depicted on the coin or contained on a certificate while the private key is concealed behind a tamper-proof hologram[13] or, less often, by a sticker or, even more rarely, engraved on the side of the coin.[14] If the hologram is opened, the private key can be swept into a wallet which transfers the crypto-currency from the coin's public address to one provided by the wallet software. Producers use holograms to make counterfeiting more difficult and to prevent unscrupulous users from copying the private key then re-selling the coin. Private keys should be kept secret as their controller 'owns' the associated crypto-currency. The producers of unfunded coins often provide a public address and private key so that buyers can self-fund the public address should they wish.

Figure 1: Casascius coin depicting the insertion and removal of a hologram.

The image above reveals how the private key is added and extracted from a coin. The first photograph shows the private key being inserted into a pit on the back of the coin. The second displays the completed coin with the private key concealed behind the sealed hologram. The third denotes the private key after the hologram has been removed. The fourth photograph indicates that the hologram has a considerably different appearance after it has been opened. This change is a security measure which reports that the private key has been accessed.

Image Credits (clockwise): Andrew Dobbins (2), Unknown (2)

Figure 2: Front and back of an iconic 1oz silver 1 BTC Casascius coin. 1. Denomination; 2. Year and weight; 3. Metal and purity; 4. Slogan; 5. Design; 6. Hologram; 7. First-bits of public address; 8. Manufacturer.

The precursors to physical Bitcoin are paper wallets and Bitbills. Interestingly, one of the first proponents of paper wallets (printing a public address and private key on paper) was Mike Caldwell, famous for Casascius coins. A June 2011 archived version of his website shows his enthusiasm for this form of secure offline storage.[15] Bitbills were introduced in May 2011 and were the first non-paper object to display bitcoin in physical form.[16] They have a hologram on top of the text of the private key which is securely sandwiched between two layers of sturdy plastic. Plastic cards are outside the scope of the *Encyclopedia* although their role in introducing the idea of physical Bitcoin should not be understated.

The first physical Bitcoin was created by Mike Caldwell of Utah. In a September 2011 post to Bitcoin Talk, he revealed that his new coins "are a REAL BITCOIN each worth 1 BTC. One side has a hologram. Underneath the hologram layer is a private key. The first 8 characters of the bitcoin address appears on each coin."[17] "Over the next two years, Caldwell issued numerous different styles of coins and bars. He was the first mover who proved that physical Bitcoin was a feasible product. His innovative stance encouraged numerous other manufacturers to enter this nascent market. By 2013, producers of funded coins included Alitin, bhCoin, Lealana, Microsoul, Nasty Mining, Recalescence Coins, and Titan.

Figure 3: Funded 1 BTC Bitbill.

Image Credits (clockwise): Unknown (all)

The Material Culture of Physical Bitcoin

At first glance, a physical Bitcoin is merely a coin. It may have an attractive visage, intriguing iconography (which often uses the 'B' for Bitcoin symbol), a colorful hologram (which is usually custom designed although some producers use a common template and add their name or logo), and text or symbol which identifies the creator. The coin might contain the text or QR code of a public address and private key. More astute observers will note that the physical aspect, while important, is but one component of the coin. In fact, physical Bitcoin are symbolically dense objects which are imbued with a multitude of ideas, beliefs, ideologies, interpretations, and psychologies.

Physical Bitcoin are a type of 'material culture' defined as "the study of artifacts of the beliefs – values, ideas, attitudes and assumptions – of a particular community or society at a given time."[18] Objects reflect the type of society in which they are created and consumed hence digital bitcoin is universal while physical Bitcoin is geographically specific which is why the majority of coins are made in the West where Bitcoin adoption is highest. (Bitcoin use is significant in China but, oddly, there are no known manufacturers of genuine coins).[19] Bitcoin is a contemporary form of material culture as the majority of evidence has been preserved online and is easily accessible in the form of articles, blogs, forum posts, discussion threads (public discussions about specific topics), and videos unlike, say, archaeological ruins that require careful excavation or dilapidated historical monuments which must be specially conserved.

Physical Bitcoin are material items that are constructed from precious metals like gold and silver or cheaper materials such as bronze and zinc alloy. Coins made from precious metals are often graded .999 (99.9% of the coin is comprised of the metal). They have a diameter, thickness, and weight, possess an insignia, text, and – if funded – report the value and type of crypto-currency.

Physical Bitcoin may be financial instruments whose bitcoin value ranges from 0.01 BTC to 1,000 BTC. The material itself is intrinsically valuable if the coin is made of silver or gold. The coins are often re-sold at a higher price. It is now common to have physical Bitcoin graded by an independent third party. At first, only Casascius coins were graded[20] but today this occurs with a variety of manufacturers.[21] This practice increases the re-sale value as long as grades are high.

Physical Bitcoin are information-rich objects which may exhort idealistic sentiments (Casascius' 'Vires en numeris' motto, Cryptolator's 'Animals' theme, and Titan's Greco-Roman warrior); depict famous personalities (Alitin's coins display Adam Smith and Jeanne D'Arc); commemorate historical events such as the collapse of Mt. Gox (Anarcoins' 'Goxxed for the last time') and the '10,000 BTC Pizza' (Bitcoin Nerd); document the statistical data of the Bitcoin network (Antana); promote an Internet meme (dogecoin from Crypto Imperator and Shibe Mint); pay homage to Satoshi Nakamoto (Ravenbit's tribute coin); endorse a visionary digital currency (Antaui's worldcoin and Finite by Design's peercoin); or represent a mining pool (Nasty Mining).

Physical Bitcoin make an ideological statement as digital Bitcoin allows consumers to choose an alternative financial system; physical Bitcoin materially denotes that ability. It takes the ideology of Bitcoin – decentralized, quasi-libertarian, pseudo-anonymous, opposed to central banking, and non-geographical – and reveals it in physical form.

Physical Bitcoin are social devices as producers interact with buyers on forums like Bitcoin Talk. Digital Bitcoin relies upon peer-to-peer nodes which route, mine, and download the blockchain while, in physical Bitcoin, this peer-to-peer model is considerably more personal and based upon interactions in forums, private messages, auctions, and the secondary (re-sale) market. Manufacturers solicit advice from the community, buyers provide feedback to producers, and sellers recommend coins to other members. Roles blur as a buyer of one coin might be a seller of another; former buyers assess their inventory and decide to sell.[22] Finally, the producers themselves are often buyers who negotiate with mints, buy holograms from reputable firms, and advertise in magazines.[23] The manufacturers and re-sellers that auction coins create a forum thread to advertise their coins, provide the starting bid, state the acceptable bid increments (for example, 0.01 BTC), and reveal the date when the auction will end.[24] All bids are public so that participants can raise their stake when their bid has been surpassed. The public nature of the auction generates a level of competition between collectors and encourages camaraderie; winners are congratulated and losers commiserated.

This social aspect of material culture is also demonstrated when forum participants, who do not necessarily know each other, engage in trades that equate to hundreds or thousands of dollars. Unlike 'conventional' financial transactions, bitcoin transfers are irreversible. Moreover, rather than drawing up formal legal contracts, negotiations and agreements occur via private message which is why reputation is paramount. Escrow providers – forum participants renowned for their trustworthiness – provide a stable and safe way to process such dealings. The buyer transmits bitcoin to the escrow agent who only sends it to the recipient once the purchaser has received their coins from the sender. The bitcoin is returned to the buyer if the sender failed to dispatch the goods. Escrow agents collect a small fee for their services akin to bitcoin miners receiving tiny transaction fees. However, escrow is often unnecessary when buyers and sellers sufficiently trust one another. The willingness for users to transmit large sums of crypto-currency which cannot be reclaimed should a transaction fail is an integral and perhaps unique aspect of the physical

Bitcoin eco-system. Trust is rarely based on the knowledge of real-world identities as parties are somewhat anonymous but instead is predicated on the trades the seller has been involved in, their conduct and demeanour on the forum, and buyers' gut feeling based on their direct participation and indirect observation of hundreds of transactions.

Physical Bitcoin are trustful commodities as producers of funded coins create the private keys and could surreptitiously retain a copy hence sensible buyers will assess the probity of the producer. Nakamoto designed Bitcoin to function without trust as the nodes and miners validate transactions, the proof-of-work cements new transactions in the blockchain, and miners append new blocks so that older blocks become immutable.[25] The physical Bitcoin world, by comparison, requires significant interpersonal trust between producers, buyers, and sellers. That said, physical Bitcoin can be password protected thanks to Bitcoin Improvement Proposal (BIP)[26] 38 designed by Mike Caldwell which enables the buyer to provide the producer with a password protected private key.[27] Sweeping funds into a wallet requires both the private key and passphrase which reduces the need to trust the manufacturer.[28] The community has not embraced Two Factor Authentication (2FA) as, instead of demanding a trustless economy, participants either buy unfunded coins (which they can self-fund and hence do not need to trust the maker), or decide that they trust a manufacturer or re-seller of funded coins. In a sense, the community has determined that not trusting their fellow peers is overrated and prefer to decide for themselves the producers and re-sellers which deserve their support.

Each producer's brand name is used to guarantee the validity of the crypto-currency referenced by the public address and the quality of the precious metal in the same way that reputable companies invoke their brand names to legitimize their products and instill the trust of their customers. The manufacturer's name or emblem is analogous to the images of monarchs and statesmen displayed on world-coins (for example, that of Queen Elizabeth II found on British and Commonwealth coins). The hologram is designed to ensure that the private key has not been compromised by corrupt actors just as the wax seals used by the nobility centuries ago guaranteed that the information in the sealed document had not been modified by hostile forces.

Physical Bitcoin are technical instruments as funded coins depict the public address and private key foregrounding the essential asymmetric cryptographic process that is core to the Bitcoin protocol.[29] They also function as a form of offline cold storage as they have no RAM or hard drive and cannot be infected with malware unlike computers and smartphones.[30]

Typology of Physical Bitcoin Producers

The physical Bitcoin movement, while incorporating revolutionary digital technology, is paradoxically traditional as it harkens back to the epoch of the artisan-craftsman. Makers' "status as artisans – principled, ideological, commerce-eschewing – gave them [artisan producers] a specialist marketing cachet, appealing very strongly to a growing segment of affluent consumers willing to seek out and pay a premium for these attributes. These artisans were able to satisfy entrepreneurial ambitions with little prejudice to product or process integrity."[31] Physical Bitcoin producers do not churn out tens of thousands of mass produced coins every year but instead produce a limited batch of tens, hundreds, or low thousands similar to artists who generate a finite number of etchings, paintings, or water-colours. Manufacturers design their own coins which reflect their artistic imprimatur.[32] Artisans have been categorized as either lifestyle- or profit-orientated. The first group want to maintain a traditional model of production, enhance the local community, and reject profit. The second type aim to increase volume, expand into new markets, and generate income. This is simplistic as the majority of artisans desire both which is certainly the case for physical Bitcoin producers. They are artisans because they have small-scale outputs, design their own coins, and are usually solo operators and are commercial because they seek profits, introduce new coins to enhance their portfolio, and constantly look for methods and strategies to enhance value.

There is therefore no clear-cut categorization although manufacturers can be broadly demarcated into commercial and hobbyist groups. Commercial producers (such as Alitin and Denarium) have a corporate structure. Denarium, for example, is part of the Finnish company Prasos Oy which owns the Bittiraha exchange and Bittimaatti ATM network.[33] Hobbyist companies (like Finite by Design and Microsoul) are run as side-businesses whose owners have a day job. Physical Bitcoin is an enjoyable way for some to earn a small additional income.

Value of Physical Bitcoin

Value is difficult to objectively define. The dollar, pound, and euro possess value because people know that they can be exchanged for goods and services at a more or less stable price. If people lose confidence in a national currency, the subjective value of that currency changes.[34] For physical Bitcoin, value is based on buyers' attachment to a particular coin at a specific moment in time. The desire to complete a collection, purchase coins with a low serial number, or acquire highly graded coins strengthens this attachment; the same psychological desire as for any collectable object. The value of drawings, paintings, sculpture, and jewellery is simply the price that the market is prepared to pay; there is no intrinsic reason why, for example, a Picasso sold for 179 million USD[35] or a Rothko for 86.9 million USD.[36] More objectively, the value of a coin is based on its crypto-currency value, metal spot value, and numismatic value (based on rarity, grade, and desirability). Objects are usually more valuable when they are scarce as mass production is infrequently correlated with desire. The creation of scarcity allows groups and individuals to influence spending patterns especially when there is competition for limited resources[37] for example when producers make small batches of, say, 100, due to a lack of funds or because they are gauging interest in a new design. The physical Bitcoin market is an ideal environment to illustrate scarcity as there is a genuine lack of the most desirable coins (some of which are 'most desirable' largely as a result of this scarcity).

The scarcity thesis is less clear for Casascius who released tens of thousands of coins. Yet, on closer inspection, the rarity principle does apply. First, Caldwell started to produce coins in late 2011 when Bitcoin was seen as nothing more than a novelty by a large portion of users. Many early recipients (especially those who were not directly interested in Bitcoin and received coins as gifts) will have discarded or otherwise lost them. Second, many collectors of high value denominations will hoard them in the hope that the bitcoin price will rise. In 2013, there were predictions that the price per BTC would top 10,000 USD[38] and those with several BTC may continue to believe this will occur. Third, Caldwell released numerous styles of coins and so, although his absolute output was considerable, the quantity of specific models is limited. Fourth, many Casascius coins were damaged when buyers peeled off the hologram and swept the funds which enhances the scarcity of coins that remain intact (the Casascius section of the *Encyclopedia* shows the number of coins that are still unopened for each batch).[39]

A key aspect that determines value in the contemporary economy is the notion of 'singularization' in which producers attempt to distinguish their outputs from those of their competitors. This means that "a good can be defined by a combination of characteristics that establish its singularity. In fact, the selected characteristics can be used to describe other goods with which relations of similitude or proximity are likely to be established. Defining a good means positioning it in a space of goods, in a system of differences and similarities, of distinct yet connected categories."[40] This is a particularly pertinent theory as the *Encyclopedia* compares and contrasts coins from different manufacturers. There are several occasions when one producer has emulated another; typically this involves an homage to and evolution of Casascius' original designs. Manufacturers often glean inspiration from extant coins while adding their own flourish.

An effective way to promote the singularization of a product is by testing. Advertisers routinely inform viewers that a study 'proved' that their product is superior to its competition. In order for results to be considered valid, the testing mechanism must appear objective to the audience otherwise the results will be considered irrelevant. This has already happened for physical Bitcoin as the community selected ANACS as the *de facto* standard for grading.[41] ANACS, established in 1972, is 'America's Oldest Grading Service'.[42] The physical Bitcoin submitted to them typically receives grades of between 60 and 70 (the higher the number, the better the grade). ANACS assess the luster (the reaction of light to the coin; a frostier luster gets a higher grade); strike (a sharper strike is better); color (for bronze and copper coins a lighter tone is best); toning (a film of sulfide can generate beautiful hues or ugly colors); wear (damage caused by friction via interaction with other coins); flaws (from the die); and the obverse (the front) of the coin.[43] Grading indicates that physical Bitcoin are effectively considered equal to coins graded for 'traditional' numismatists who collect 'conventional' world-coins. Grading is a burgeoning industry exemplified by the fact that, in August 2015, ANACS created a specific category for the submission of physical Bitcoin.[44]

Figure 4: Casascius coin graded 'MS-69' by ANACS.

Coins are distinguished by their materials (such as copper, gold, silver, zinc, brass [an alloy of copper and zinc], or bronze [an alloy of copper and tin]), images, and text. Manufacturers differentiate themselves from one another by providing accoutrements such as certificates of authenticity, presentation boxes, and stickers. Coins with a defect may command a premium as spelling mistakes, imperfectly aligned holograms, and misaligned text can potentially enhance value.[45] Yet the overall quality cannot be poor; the community wants uniqueness but not at the expense of shoddy workmanship and inferior production techniques.

Funded coins are set apart from unfunded coins while those that are funded are further qualified by the type of crypto-currency. Bitcoin is the standard but coins have also been funded with a variety of other digital currencies which include litecoin (Lealana), dogecoin (Crypto Imperator), monero (Cryptonic),[46] and worldcoin (Antaui).[47] The value of currency provides an additional point of difference. The majority of recently manufactured coins have values of 0.01 BTC, 0.1 BTC, 0.25 BTC, 0.5 BTC, and 1 BTC which makes TGBEX's 20 BTC and 50 BTC coins really stand out.[48] Pre-2013 coins had higher denominations due to the lower value of a BTC when exchanged for national currencies.

Image Credits: Scott Barnett

Regulation of Physical Bitcoin

In the US, companies that transmit money must register as a Money Service Business (MSB). A FinCEN (Financial Crimes Enforcement Network)[49] *Factsheet* notes that "[t]o meet the definition of an MSB, a person must conduct more than $1,000 in business with one person in one or more transactions [...] on any one day. However, there is one exception. No activity threshold applies to the definition of money transmitter. A person that engages as a business in the transfer of funds is a money transmitter and an MSB, regardless of the amount of transfer activity."[50]

On 18 March 2013, FinCEN issued guidance entitled *Application of FinCEN's Regulations to Persons Administering, Exchanging, or Using Virtual Currencies*.[51] It explained that the regulations apply to those who create, buy, and sell digital currency. An 'administrator' issues and redeems digital currency; manufacturers who fund coins transmit crypto-currency to public addresses which makes them administrators and means they must register as an MSB. The guidance showed that crypto-currency providers are not immune from regulation and, that as money transmitters, they cannot legally engage in any transaction of any amount whatsoever without registering.

In November 2013, FinCEN informed Mike Caldwell that he was a money transmitter and must register as an MSB.[52] Caldwell decided to stop funding coins as he did not "want the] compliance hassle of being a money transmitter (this was a hobby project meant to promote awareness – moving money was never an objective)."[53] Other manufacturers like Lealana also terminated funding as a direct result of the letter received by Caldwell.[54] The move from funded to unfunded resulted from the fear that FinCEN would accuse producers of being unlicensed money transmitters. Physical Bitcoin companies could register as an MSB, as Caldwell initially did,[55] but registration forces companies to comply with Anti-Money Laundering (AML) policies and potentially file Suspicious Activity Reports (SARs) on their customers which is likely to be off-putting to buyers who often prefer to remain somewhat anonymous.[56] Registration as an MSB is simple; it is the legal obligations that registration imposes which are onerous and expensive. The easiest solution for American companies is simply not to directly fund their coins while non-American manufacturers often refuse to ship pre-funded coins to the US. Denarium, for example, will not send their pre-funded 0.01 BTC coin to the US even though its value at the time of writing is less than 3 USD.[57] Coins credited with bitcoin were not the only ones affected as American manufacturers that referenced other crypto-currencies also terminated funding. Finite by Design, for example, stopped providing a funded 10 peercoin model.[58]

The transition from pre-funded to unfunded means that producers that continue to pre-fund coins are in the minority which makes their products stand out. Funded coins from manufacturers who subsequently stopped funding (such as Lealana) command a premium on the secondary market. To obtain pre-funded coins, Americans must participate in a 'group buy' in which a non-American based collector buys pre-funded coins in bulk from the supplier and sends them to a contact in the US to distribute the funded coins State-side.[59] This demonstrates the premium that collectors attach to producer funded coins and displays the workaround necessitated by the American regulatory attitude towards money transmitters. The collector who arranges the group buy must publicize his plan, obtain the names and addresses of interested parties, order coins from the producer, pay for them, receive them in the mail, package and post them to customers in the destination country, receive payments from collectors, and potentially deal with lost or delayed shipments. This is a time-consuming endeavour which demands a significant level of organizational skill. There is no personal economic profit or reward for this service to the physical Bitcoin community other than a feeling that one has engaged in a worthwhile task and the knowledge that such an act significantly enhances one's reputation.

Collectors of Physical Bitcoin

There are a number of reasons why collectors became interested in physical Bitcoin. One commenced by buying three Casascius brass coins as he felt this was the easiest way to acquire and hold digital bitcoin. Until recently, purchasing bitcoin was a significant challenge to many; obtaining funded Casascius coins from eBay was an obvious solution and explains why so many coins were redeemed shortly after purchase. This collector was worried that bitcoin stored on his computer would be hacked or he would lose his wallet's private keys. Another heard negative stories about the collapse of the Japan-based Mt. Gox exchange and believed that funded coins were a more secure way to hold crypto-currency. He also realised that the only way to redeem the bitcoin was to remove the hologram which would, in his opinion, destroy the coin. He knew that keeping the coins intact would ensure he did not spend the bitcoin. One bought dozens of Casascius coins when each bitcoin was worth very little. He believed that, if the price of bitcoin rose, he would make a substantial profit. Another was a miner who speculated that Bitcoin might collapse and used his mining profits to purchase physical Bitcoin in order to memorialize his experience. In these cases, as for the majority of participants, the first purchase quickly spiralled into more intensive collecting bolstered by the rapidly increasing number of manufacturers and styles of coin on offer.

One thought was whether collectors had previously systematically acquired other objects as, if so, they may have developed a 'collector's mentality' of generating an ever more impressive assortment, bartering goods, cataloguing and arranging items, and perhaps displaying their purchases. One was a 'silver stacker' who bought Norfed silver coins[60] before starting his journey with physical Bitcoin; another collated American coins, comic books, autographs, and Star Wars memorabilia. A different connoisseur used to obtain world-coins, paper money, and stamps but his collections were fragmented. In contrast, he meticulously documents his physical Bitcoin. The reverse was less often the case although one person procured Bitcoin and then became enamoured of traditional coins particularly Chinese 'silver pandas'.[61] It is clear that most collectors had a psychological desire to gather items long before they heard of Bitcoin. Physical Bitcoin have similarities with objects like world-coins, stamps, and silver coins: they can be arranged in collections; have economic worth; can be re-sold on a secondary market; are portable; and have hierarchies of value which privilege coins from certain manufacturers, made from specific materials, or those that are most scarce.

Some collectors target a select number of manufacturers while others widely purchase from both established and new producers. The most popular make is Casascius; other well-known brands are Crypto Imperator, Cryptolator, Denarium, Lealana, Microsoul, and Ravenbit. The affection for Casascius derives from its status as the originator of funded coins, the wide variety of outputs in various styles and denominations, the lack of new coins (which is unlikely to change since Caldwell has effectively retired from the physical Bitcoin scene), the probability that many coins have been lost or destroyed as they were received when bitcoin was worth a negligible amount, and the intense competition for the few coins that become available on the secondary market. An aficionado of Crypto Imperator praised the high quality precious metal look, attractive and complex hologram, and limited mintage. At times, collectors had their esoteric favorites: a devotee of the obscure MJB Monetary Metals supported the brand because it was one of the first coins made, was produced in small batches, and tarnishes easily (so his good quality coins are rarer as the majority of other collectors' coins may have been badly tarnished due to improper handling and storage). This individual also appreciated the overlooked SerpCoin as the producer applied Caldwell's vision of using Casascius aluminum blanks to make wallets while the small mintage implies that this was a hobby rather than a serious business venture. A different collector advocated Titan as he enjoyed the classical iconography of the obverse, the high quality finish, and the premium material.

The majority of collectors agree that the most desirable coins are pre-funded by the manufacturer; unfunded coins that are funded by the buyer before shipping are slightly less prestigious. In the latter model, the producer must verify that the coin's public address has been funded before posting the coin. A variation is unfunded coins which can be funded by the buyer. This distinction between producer pre-funded, buyer funded, and unfunded coins is insignificant to many collectors who consider all methods equally respectable. One collector did not fund unfunded coins but stressed that doing so corroborates the age of the coin since the exact date of funding is recorded in perpetuity on the public blockchain. This person also asserted that the minimum amount for funded coins should be 0.1 BTC; anything less, he believed, was too small. One collector, who is partial to self-assembly coins, accidentally damaged two different models as he attempted to construct them. His goal was to insert a private key, affix a hologram, and fund the associated public address to the value depicted on the coin. He stressed that funding DIY coins places a small amount of bitcoin outside his immediate reach thus forcing him to save it. Moreover, he asserts that the currency is totally secure since he himself creates and appends the private key. Multiple people asserted that the downside to self-generated private keys for DIY coins is that it is hard to re-sell the coin as potential buyers must have total faith that the seller did not retain a copy of the private key. It was suggested that, in order to be referred to as 'coins', crypto-currency themed pieces of metal must contain a private key (or have the potential to have one added) and thus have the capability to be funded or else they should be regarded as novelty tokens. The *Encyclopedia* makes the same distinction: 'coins' that are 'wallets' include or could include a private key while 'rounds' are not sold with a private key and are not constructed in a way that they can have one appended by the buyer.

All aficionados appreciate a serial number of 10 and under as it implies that they were one of the first to acquire a specific model. One collector stressed that the serial number only adds value if the serialized coins are part of a large batch which distinguishes them from non-serialized coins. Errors only enhance value if they amplify the rarity of a coin. A collector retained a Microsoul 'zombie' coin which was later recalled by the producer as he felt that the rarity of the error might someday make it valuable. A producer's first coin often has an error as they are learning to create professional outputs; such coins are valuable not only because of the error itself but also because they reflect a manufacturer's first coin. This represents the desire to own the 'first' coin in a series (assuming, of course, that the manufacturer made multiple different styles of coin). 'Error fatigue' occurs if too many coins have errors and hence the concept is no longer exceptional. In conventional coin production, errors are caught quickly so only a few substandard coins are inadvertently released. Physical Bitcoin producers cannot afford the same quality control standards thus errors often remain undiscovered until the full batch has been generated. This means that some error coins are not particularly rare. One collector asserted that the secondary market over-inflated the economic value of Casascius 2011 Error Coins, of which 4,160 were made, primarily because the hologram contained a spelling error.

Collectors are increasingly dealing with graded coins. Originally, only the most illustrious brands were graded although it is now conventional to grade any coin of high quality.[62] One collector replaces his lowest graded Casascius coins with those possessing higher grades while another believes that only Casascius and selected Lealana coins should be graded; assessing less distinguished coins is, he felt, somewhat 'gimmicky' and not financially sensible as paying the grading fee for a coin worth a small amount would not sufficiently increase its value to make grading worthwhile. Additionally, it is now the norm for producers to deliver coins in secure air tight cases negating the need to pay a grading service to preserve the coins (Casascius coins, in contrast, were rarely shipped in plastic coin protectors). It was argued that it would be disadvantageous to sell ungraded Casascius coins as the market expects graded versions; un-graded coins are consequently valued significantly lower. Some collectors re-grade their already graded coins by cracking the slab and re-submitting the coin.[63] The mantra may well be 'buy the coin not the slab' yet, in reality, the slab (or, more accurately, its accompanying grade) is highly important when determining the value of the most renowned brands.

There are two broad groups of collectors. The first targets the most esteemed manufacturers and aims to create a collection based on quality and rarity which will eventually be worth many tens or hundreds of thousands of dollars. The second wishes to collect as many different coins as possible and owns numerous obscure coins but not ones that necessarily command respect. One connoisseur's long-term goal is to generate a collection based on scarcity and high grades in the hope that it will eventually be worth a life-changing amount. This person no longer buys from new manufacturers but uses revenue from disposing of less illustrious items to purchase early issues (like Casascius and Lealana), highly graded coins, those of low mintages, and error coins. By comparison, a different aficionado aims to collect every coin created (with the exception of the very expensive Casascius coins). He has almost 200 unique coins and is continually appending more. He hopes that, in time, the market will acknowledge that his collection is economically worthy due to its breadth and variety. However, his primary goal is to complete his collection as he derives joy from collecting objects. It is part of what makes him who he is. Collectors therefore 'profit' both economically and psychologically and it is important not to overstate the economic aspects as many – perhaps most – collectors want to have fun expanding or refining their intake rather than trying to make serious money. The majority of those who have come to regard physical Bitcoin as a business simultaneously consider it a hobby.

Enthusiasts sell their least desired coins to raise funds for more expensive purchases. Traders and flippers employ different tactics as the former holds valuable coins for months or years before selling them while the latter retains coins for a matter of weeks. A trader may bulk buy ten coins, sell eight, and keep two. A flipper, on the other hand, is looking for a quick yet insubstantial profit. Sometimes an individual buys a large amount of coins with a bulk discount from a producer and will later sell them for significantly higher prices once the coins sold directly by the manufacturer have become difficult to obtain.
Collectors comprise part of a global hobbyist network centered on the 'Economy – Marketplace – Goods – Collectibles' section of Bitcoin Talk.[64] One collector noted that he

has made new friends from all over the world. Interestingly, he connects the tangibility of physical Bitcoin (in comparison to digital Bitcoin) to the tangibility of human collectors (in contrast to anonymous computerized nodes on the peer-to-peer network). Many collectors spend several hours each week browsing the forum, trading their coins, contacting buyers and re-sellers, and participating in threads. One scours new posts in order to locate novel coins for sale; he then immediately contacts the supplier to request the lowest possible serial number (should the coin be serialized).

The more serious collectors securely store their coins off-site in safety deposit boxes. One kept a few coins in his home in a fire proof safe. These coins are no longer novelty items but objets d'art that are appreciating in value and are treated as such. One hobbyist places his coins into a Quadrum display case and studies them from time to time to appreciate their artistry.[65] They are accessible to him but not on display for visitors. Another arranges his coins on stands so they can be viewed. He opens the slab of graded coins with pliers as he asserts that they obscure the coins' features. His casual attitude towards the slab indicates that not all supporters of physical Bitcoin regard grading as paramount; some prefer to simply display their coins and consider the slab an irksome obstacle.

There was some debate about whether customers should know the identity of producers. Forum participants use 'handles' rather than their real names. The need to assess the legitimacy of manufacturers depends on whether they fund their coins and, if so, the amount. More than one collector was unconcerned if a low value funded coin was compromised. Another stressed that new producers could offer a DIY coin along with funded coins to build-up trust and legitimacy. That said, the identity of the owners of the majority of funded manufacturers – Alitin, Casascius, Denarium, Lealana, Microsoul, TGBEX, and Titan among others – are publicly available. In terms of the secondary market, a high quality photograph of an intact hologram suggests that the coin has not been exploited. Collectors must trust each other when re-selling coins; one seller suggests that new buyers spend sufficient time developing trust by making small trades before buying or selling more renowned works like high denomination Casascius coins or valuable physical Bitcoin made from pure silver.

Although not mentioned by these collectors, the initial relevance of Casascius, the first physical Bitcoin, was their utility in depicting a 'tangible' Bitcoin able to introduce the uninitiated to the subject. As such, they functioned as a 'conversation starter' that could be gifted to a friend or work colleague. Those who received a metal coin with an associated digital value were likely to investigate further and thus learn about the technology that makes Bitcoin possible. Low-cost physical Bitcoin, whether pre-funded or unfunded, is still marketed as an item that will attract attention when placed in a public area such as on a shelf or coffee table.

Another intriguing rationale for purchasing funded coins is as a hedge against a possible failure of the Bitcoin network. In such a case, if Bitcoin collapsed and crypto-currency became all but worthless, the buyer would not lose his entire investment. For example, the value of bitcoin in a 1 BTC Casascius coin might be the equivalent of 500 USD. If bitcoin lost 99 percent of its worth and the value of the currency reduced to a mere 5 USD, the market value of the coin would not drop as dramatically as a substantial portion of the original purchase price derives from factors other than the BTC value.

Structure of the Encyclopedia

This work covers physical Bitcoin manufactured between summer 2011 and early 2016. 'Coins' and 'bars' contain a private key and have either been pre-funded by the producer, by the purchaser in advance of receipt, or can potentially be funded by the buyer. They include coins that do not contain a private key but have the ability to have one added by the purchaser. The crucial aspect, whether these coins are producer funded, buyer funded, unfunded, or self-assembled is that they meet the definition of a wallet since they come with a private key or one can be added. These coins have a hologram (or, less commonly, a sticker) which conceals the private key (except in the case of Alitin coins which have the private key engraved on the side of the coin). By comparison, 'rounds' do not include a private key and do not possess the flat bare surface area (let alone a private key pit) necessary to append a private key. They are, in effect, tokens rather than wallets. The *Encyclopedia* focuses on coins, bars, and rounds that are made from metal and therefore excludes paper wallets[66] and plastic cards like Bitbills, Crypto Coin Wallet Cards,[67] and Prypto.[68]

Bitcoin is the original and dominant crypto-currency which inspired the creation of other digital currencies and it has thus become conventional to refer to non-bitcoin currencies as 'alternative'. The term is not meant to pass judgement on the legitimacy or value of these 'alt currencies'. Litecoin, for example, is barely considered an 'alt' and its many supporters consider it to be as legitimate as Bitcoin. The *Encyclopedia* does not privilege bitcoin and thus depicts coins endowed with a wide variety of 'alt' currencies including dogecoin, litecoin, monero, primecoin, and worldcoin.

Figure 5: Popular coins of the five Types: from top left PF – Pre-Funded (Casascius); BF – Buyer Funded (Lealana); UF – Unfunded (Cryptolator); DIY – Do It Yourself (Silver Wallets); RD – Round (Anarcoins).

The description for each entry displays:

Manufacturer: the official name of the producer.
Make: the name of the coin provided by the producer along with any nicknames.
Type: is divided into five sections.
  Pre-Funded (PF) – the coin is directly funded by the manufacturer.
  Buyer Funded (BF) – the buyer directly funds the coin before it is shipped.
  Unfunded (UF) – shipped with a private key but without loaded value.
  Do It Yourself (DIY) – the customer can affix a private key and hologram.
  Rounds – the object does not have the capacity to contain a private key and hologram.
Year: when the coin was first advertised for sale.
Denomination: the value of crypto-currency displayed on the coin.
Material: this may be silver or gold or a less prestigious material such as brass, copper, or zinc. Specific types of a metal such as Antique Copper or Merlin Gold are mentioned.
Mintage: the number of coins produced; sub-mintages are given when appropriate.
Diameter: the width of the coin.
Thickness: the distance between the top and bottom of the coin.

Image Credits (clockwise): Casascius (2), Elias Ahonen (2), Howard Kesselman, Silver Wallets, Howard Kesselman, Elias Ahonen (3)

Weight: in grams (and ounces or troy ounces when appropriate).
Country: the location of the manufacturer.
Highest Grade: provided solely for Casascius which is the most commonly graded producer. The grade significantly affects the coins' value in the secondary market. The grade is the highest that has been publicized.

Depending on the producer and coin, each entry may explore the biography of the manufacturer, detail the coin's appearance (in particular any memorable or unusual features), reveal its historical significance, and analyze the design, iconography, hologram, colors, size, and weight. There are photographs of the front and back of each coin. The photographer has, on occasion, strategically concealed the public address to preserve his privacy.

Conclusion

Physical Bitcoin are imbued with a wealth of meaning that complements their material appeal. Elias and I are confident that the *Encyclopedia* is a worthy attempt to introduce these coins and their makers to the mainstream audience that they richly deserve. Simultaneously, our aim is to thank the physical Bitcoin community for their innovation and industriousness which has enabled this novel industry to thrive. The production, transmission, and consumption of these objects has created and solidified a community which promotes both digital and physical Bitcoin within an Internet culture of trust.

I would like to conclude by suggesting that physical Bitcoin possess a 'spiritual' aspect. This may be considered somewhat unusual as these technological objects are rational, precise, unemotional, amoral, and universal. Yet I cannot conceive of a better way to conceptualize physical Bitcoin. The ideas denoted by physical coins – independence, community, innovation, progress, and beauty – are values that are spiritually pure. I believe it to be an appropriate, uplifting, and optimistic way to summarize an industry whose practitioners – manufacturers, buyers, re-sellers, graders, and commentators – have not only inaugurated an entirely new enterprise but also generated a community that is dedicated to the values and aspirations inherent to Bitcoin.

Matthew J. Rippon PhD
March 2016

Endnotes

1. Nakamoto is anonymous so there is no way to confirm his gender. Satoshi could be a man, woman, group of people, company, organization, or government agency. 'He' presented himself as male.
2. "Bitcoin: A Peer-to-Peer Electronic Cash System" Satoshi Nakamoto (2008). Link: https://bitcoin.org/bit coin.pdf
3. The protocol is 'Bitcoin' while the currency is 'bitcoin'.
4. Miners perform proof-of-work (POW) exercises on the 'candidate block' of unconfirmed transactions. Miners use the computational power of their hardware to rapidly hash the candidate block and generate a hash below a defined number known as the difficulty target. The first miner to achieve this is rewarded with 25 BTC at the time of writing.
5. Two excellent guides to Bitcoin are "Mastering Bitcoin: Unlocking Digital Cryptocurrencies" Andreas Antonopoulos (2014) and "Bitcoin for the Befuddled" Conrad Barski and Chris Wilmer (2014).
6. "Silk Road: The Untold Story" *Wired* 23 May 2015. Link: http://www.wired.com/2015/05/silk-road-unt old-story/
7. The bitcoin price rose from 13 USD on 1 January 2013 to 1,120 USD on 29 November 2013.
8. "Bitcoin Isn't the Future of Money – It's Either a Ponzi Scheme or a Pyramid Scheme" *Washington Post* 8 June 2015. Link: https://www.washingtonpost.com/news/wonkblog/wp/2015/06/08/bitcoin-isnt-the-future-of-money-its-either-a-ponzi-scheme-or-a-pyramid-scheme/
9. Bitcoin 2.0 businesses employ the blockchain to – among other uses – issue smart contracts, validate identities, and notarize documents.
10. That said, Mike Caldwell, founder of Casascius coins, appears in the documentary "The Rise and Rise of Bitcoin" (2014) for three minutes and 19 seconds from 45:57. Link: http://www.imdb.com/title/tt2821314/ He discusses his filming experience at https://casascius.wordpress.com/2013/05/19/casascius-coin-production-featured-in-the-rise-and-rise-of-bitcoin/
11. This is not to suggest that physical Bitcoin enthusiasts do not research coins. I merely note that, until now, there has not been a comprehensive catalogue which provides data and photographs on all known manufacturers and their products.
12. The prefix is typically the first eight digits of a coin's public address. The first character is '1' and each of the next seven characters can be one of 58 examples. As such, there are a total of 2,207,984,167,552 possibilities which means that the likelihood of finding two public addresses with the same eight first characters is remote. The full public address can either be discovered by entering the first characters on a blockchain website like https://btc.blockr.io/ or is shown on an enclosed certificate.
13. Casascius holograms were successfully compromised at the DEF CON hacker convention in August 2013. Caldwell immediately took measures to ensure that future coins were tamper-proof. "Casascius Physical Bitcoins Cracked at Defcon" Link: http://codinginmysleep.com/casascius-physical-bi coins-cracked-at-defcon/ "Defcon 21: Successful Compromise of the Hologram Reported" Link: https://casascius.wordpress.com/2013/08/04/defcon-21-successful-compromise-of-the-hologram-reported/
14. This is only the case for Alitin. Link: http://www.alitinmint.com/Home/About
15. "Paper Bitcoin Wallet" Link: https://web.archive.org/web/20110629211014/http://www.casascius.com/
16. "Introducing Bitbills!" *Bitcoin Talk* 9 May 2011. Link: https://bitcointalk.org/index.php?topic=7724
17. "CASASCIUS PHYSICAL BITCOIN – In Stock Now! (pic)" *Bitcoin Talk* 6 September 2011. Link: https://bitcointalk.org/index.php?topic=41892
18. "Mind in Matter: An Introduction to Material Culture Theory and Method" Jules David Prown (1982) *Winterthur Portfolio* 17: 1 p. 1.
19. Chinese mints make coins for Western producers but infrequently make their own original physical Bitcoin. The only known examples are Geek Bitcoin and Chinese Businessman.
20. "First Ever Graded Casascius Coins?" *Bitcoin Talk* 24 April 2013. Link: https://bitcointalk.org/index.php?topic=186098

21. "Grading Coins – A Few Basic Questions" *Bitcoin Talk* 27 July 2015. Link: https://bitcointalk.org/index.php?topic=1136216
22. For example, "[WTS] Casascius, Lealana, CI, Veri, Antaui *OPEN FOR BUSINESS*" *Bitcoin Talk* 3 August 2015. Link: https://bitcointalk.org/index.php?topic=1142211
23. Caldwell advertised in all 22 print issues of *Bitcoin Magazine.*
24. A producer auction is "Lealana Auction" *Bitcoin Talk* 7 February 2015. Link: https://bitcointalk.org/index.php?topic=948952 and a re-seller auction is "Casascius 25 BTC coin" Bitcoin Talk 1 August 2015. Link: https://bitcointalk.org/index.php?topic=1140324
25. Nakamoto stated (p. 1) that "[w]hat is needed is an electronic payment system based on cryptographic proof instead of trust, allowing any two willing parties to transact directly with each other without the need for a trusted third party."
26. Bitcoin Improvement Proposals (BIPs) are modifications to the Bitcoin protocol or information about suggested amendments. Link: https://en.bitcoin.it/wiki/Bitcoin_Improvement_Proposals
27. "Casascius" Link: https://casascius.com/2factor/
28. Some physical Bitcoin producers create their own two factor schemes. While this does secure bitcoin from interlopers, it in no way negates the need for buyers to trust the manufacturers.
29. Wallet software uses entropy to generate the private key and public key. The resulting public key is hashed with SHA-256 and RIPEMD-160, the hexadecimal prefix 0x01 and checksum is added, and the result is encoded with Base58Check to produce the public address.
30. "Bitcoins, Other Digital Currencies Stolen in Massive 'Pony' Botnet Attack" *PCWorld* 24 February 2014. Link: http://www.pcworld.com/article/2101260/bitcoins-other-digital-currencies-stolen-in-massive-pony-botnet-attack.html
31. "Lifestyle, Growth, or Community Involvement? The Balance of Goals of UK Artisan Food Producers" Angela Tregear (2005) *Entrepreneurship and Regional Development* 17: 1 p. 12.
32. "Coin Making Guide: From Sketch to Strike" Jonathan Frammingham (2015).
33. "Services – Prasos Oy" Link: https://prasos.fi/?page_id=97
34. For example, in 2009, Zimbabwe issued a 100 trillion Z$ note.
35. "Picasso Painting Breaks Record For Most Expensive Artwork Sold at Auction" *The Guardian* 12 May 2015. Link: http://www.theguardian.com/artanddesign/2015/may/12/pablo-picasso-work-sets-record-for-most-expensive-artwork-sold-at-auction
36. "Mark Rothko Work Sold For Record $86.9m at Auction" *BBC* 9 May 2012. Link: http://www.bbc.co.uk/news/world-us-canada-18001432
37. "Influence: Science and Practice" Robert Cialdini (2001) pp. 203-232.
38. "BitcoinSpeculation.net – A Collection of Bitcoin Price Predictions and Speculation" Link: http://bitcoinspeculation.net/
39. "Casascius Bitcoin Analyzer" Link: http://casascius.uberbills.com/
40. "The Economy of Qualities" Michel Callon, Cécile Méadel, and Vololona Rabeharisoa (2002) *Economy and Society* 31: 2 p. 198.
41. The two other major American coin graders – Professional Coin Grading Service and Independent Coin Graders – refuse to certify physical Bitcoin. The Coin Grading Service UK does grade physical Bitcoin but, confusingly, has a proprietary grading system. The vast majority of collectors, including those in the UK, use ANACS.
42. "ANACS – America's Oldest Coin Authentication and Grading Service" Link: http://www.anacs.com/
43. "Coin Grading and Professional Third-Party Grading Services" *ANACS* (undated) pp. 9-11. Link: http://www.anacs.com/PDFFiles/ANACS_Brochure.pdf
44. "Submission Form" Link: http://www.anacs.com/PDFFiles/submissionform.pdf
45. For example, "[WTS] Casascius coins – 1 BTC 2011 Error coin – .5 Brass 2013 – 1 BTC Silver 2013" *Bitcoin Talk* 14 June 2015. Link: https://bitcointalk.org/index.php?topic=1089616
46. "Cryptonic PHYSICAL MONEROj for SALE" *Bitcoin Talk* 10 March 2015. Link: https://bitcointalk.org/index.php?topic=984034

47. "[Make Offer] Antaui, 5WDC, 1 Oz. Silver Coins... for Nxt" *Nxt Forum* 24 April 2014. Link: https://nxt forum.org/trading-exchanges/antaui-5wdc-1-oz-silver-coins-for-nxt/
48. "Pricing | TGBEX" Link: http://www.tgbex.com/pricing/
49. FinCEN is part of the U.S. Department of the Treasury.
50. "Money Services Business Registration Factsheet" *FinCEN* (undated). Link: http://www.fincen.gov/finan cial_institutions/msb/pdf/FinCENfactsheet.pdf
51. "Application of FinCEN's Regulations to Persons Administering, Exchanging, or Using Virtual Currencies" *FinCEN* 18 March 2013. Link: http://fincen.gov/statutes_regs/guidance/pdf/FIN-2013-G001.pdf
52. "U.S. Government Nastygram Shuts Down One-Man Bitcoin Mint" *Wired* 12 December 2013. Link: http://www.wired.com/2013/12/casascius/
53. "Re: [WTB/WTS] Casascius Holo Error / Collectible Marketplace" *Bitcoin Talk* 17 March 2014. Link: https://bitcointalk.org/index.php?topic=214589.msg5738972#msg5738972
54. "LEALANA PHYSICAL BTC & LTC RESUMING SALES (UNFUNDED)" *Bitcoin Talk* 16 May 2014. Link: https://bitcointalk.org/index.php?topic=610924
55. "Re: 2013-12-12 Wired – U.S. Government Nastygram Shuts Down One-Man Bitcoin Mint" *Bitcoin Talk* 15 December 2013. Link: https://bitcointalk.org/index.php?topic=368431.msg3972512#msg3972512
56. "Guidance on Preparing A Complete & Sufficient Suspicious Activity Report Narrative" *FinCEN* November 2003. Link: http://www.fincen.gov/statutes_regs/files/sarnarrcompletguidfinal_112003.pdf
57. "Denarium Bitcoin | Affordable Physical Bitcoins" Link: https://denarium.com/
58. "f*D | Rare .999 Fine Silver Crypto Proofs" *Peercoin Talk* December 28 2013. Link: https://www.peer cointalk.org/index.php?topic=1782
59. "[USA/CANADA GROUP BUY] Denarium Silver 1 BTC Coins" *Bitcoin Talk* 23 October 2015. Link: https://bitcointalk.org/index.php?topic=1218530
60. "Norfed lovers stackers space (Page 1)" Link: http://forums.silverstackers.com/topic-13835-norfed-lov ers-stackers-space.html
61. "Chinese Silver Panda" Link: https://en.wikipedia.org/wiki/Chinese_Silver_Panda
62. For example, Supernet coins, which were only released in June 2015, had been graded by December. "1st Edition Supernet Coins – Silver/Antique/Gold" *Bitcoin Talk* 21 June 2015. Link: https://bitcointalk.org/ index.php?topic=1096184.msg13178175#msg13178175
63. "Physical Crypto General Discussion" *Bitcoin Talk* 21 July 2015. Link: https://bitcointalk.org/index. php?topic=1129862
64. "Collectibles" Link: https://bitcointalk.org/index.php?board=217
65. "Quadrum coin cases" Link: http://www.coingallery.co.uk/quadrum-coin-cases-36-c.asp
66. "Bitcoin Paper Wallet Generator: Print Offline Tamper-Resistant Addresses" Link: https://bitcoinpaper wallet.com/
67. "Crypto Coin Wallet Cards – Bitcoin, Litecoin, and Ppcoin Paper Wallets" Link: https://www.cryptocoin walletcards.com/
68. "Prypto: About Prypto" Link: https://prypto.com/?pg=qLSeries 1s6rPyeLp5g

Endnotes with hyperlinks are available online at:
http://www.coinfirm.org/Endnotes.pdf

Encyclopedia of Physical Bitcoins and Crypto-Currencies

Alitin Mint

Alitin Mint is among the most unique and prestigious manufacturers of physical Bitcoins. Unlike other physical crypto-currencies, Alitin coins do not have any kind of hologram seal. Instead, the private key is etched directly into the side of the coin and it is then placed in a secure slab that covers the sides. In this way, the coin is fully funded but a hologram does not take up space on the coin. Redeeming the coin requires the breaking of the slab, but unlike the case with holograms there is no physical change to the coin whatsoever. The public key is tastefully etched onto the backside of the coins. A concern that was brought to light regarding the engraving of private keys was the possibility of a 'hacker' using an ultrasound or MRI machine to discern the characters inside the slab. This was taken seriously, and it was confirmed by a radiologist that such a feat was not possible with current technology.

The coins are created by John B. Andelin, a self-taught 'Presidential Sculptor' whose work includes a nine foot statue of former US president George H. W. Bush made from a 19,600 pound block of Colorado Yule marble. His other works include "The Dawning of a Brighter Day" life-sized statue of Joseph Smith (the founder of Mormonism), amongst other religious inspired works. Mr. Andelin is a pathologist, and uses his expert knowledge of human anatomy to perfect his sculptures. Unrelated to his work with sculpture and Bitcoin, he has written "Evolution: Mask of Science" in which he claims to refute the scientific concept of evolutionary biology and according to the book description, "eviscerates the entire treatise of Darwinism".[1]

Each coin made by Alitin is made in the honor of an individual who has somehow benefited humanity in a selfless manner. Due to Alitin's unique design eschewing holograms and their emphasis in creating obviously respectable pieces of art, they are uniquely placed to attract interest from serious numismatists who may not have any initial interest in Bitcoin. Indeed it is Alitin Mint's hope to spread worldwide interest of Bitcoin in this way, which would most certainly also bring a highly increased collector interest in physical crypto-currencies. Alitin takes the legal issues regarding 'money transmitting' faced by Casascius seriously. In fact, it is a subsidiary of a licensed money services business with fully valid money transmitter licensing. It is interesting to note that according to their website, Alitin donates a portion of all proceeds to The Bitcoin Foundation. This organization that has become quite controversial among many Bitcoin users, due to questions of centralization and bias.

Image Credits: Alitin Mint

1. "Evolution: Mask of Science Kindle Edition" Link: http://www.amazon.ca/Evolution-Mask-Science-J-B-Andelin-ebook/dp/B00PL7WOQK

Alitin Mint

2013 Adam Smith Limited 1st Edition

Manuf.	Alitin Mint
Year	2013
Denom.	2 BTC
Type	PF
Mintage	600
Material	.999 Silver
Diameter	44.45 mm
Thickness	5 mm
Weight	2 ozt
Country	USA

Alitin's first coin represents Adam Smith, whose "revolutionary philosophies have permeated monetary policy throughout the industrialized world. As bitcoin enthusiasts, all of us appreciate the value of the free market system, particularly as it pertains to commodity and currency trade. So for these reasons, we are proud to introduce our inaugural coin.[1] The first funded physical Bitcoin (in a coin format) without a hologram of any kind, it is also notable for being the first coin to be funded with 2 BTC as opposed to 1, 3, or 5.

Image Credits (clockwise): Howard Kesselman (all)

1. "Coins" Link: http://www.alitinmint.com/Coins

Alitin Mint

2014 Jeanne D'Arc Limited 1st Edition

Manuf.	Alitin Mint
Year	2014
Denom.	1 BTC
Type	PF
Mintage	600
Material	.999 Silver
Diameter	44.45 mm
Thickness	5 mm
Weight	2 ozt
Country	USA

The face of this coin features an expertly crafted image of Joan D' Arc, and is arguably among the most visually striking physical Bitcoins to date from an artistic perspective. The back contains French symbolism in reference to Joan D' Arc, including fleur-de-lis and a Cross of Lorraine. Like the Adam Smith coin, the Bitcoin 'B' symbol is displayed on the lower backside. The public key is etched onto the upper right of the backside in small print, although the coin slab also features a QR code for more convenient checking of the balance.

Image Credits (clockwise): Howard Kesselman (all)

Anarcoins

Anarcoins is run by Jonathan Frammingham of the UK, with 'Anar' referring to anarcho-capitalism which is an influential viewpoint in the Bitcoin world. In addition to producing physical crypto rounds and bars, he is the author of the book *Coin Making Guide – From Sketch to Strike* which is particularly relevant to hobbyists such as himself who are looking to create their own custom coins. The book is pictured on the bottom right.

Anarcoins launched a 'commemorative (commiserative) coin' to memorialize the infamous 'Mt. Gox Crash' in which 850,000 BTC (worth over $450,000,000 at the time) was lost by thousands of individuals holding bitcoin in Mt. Gox. While much controversy surrounds the events that lead to the exchange's insolvency, there is no doubt that it had a devastating effect on the bitcoin community with about 7% of all bitcoins ever created (and over 10% of all circulating bitcoin) at the time being lost. Such a traumatic event is no doubt a formative event for bitcoin as a currency, and the thinking behind Anarcoins was that a round to signify the event was an appropriate way to create a historical record and attempt to 'console' those who lost great sums of money.

Anarcoins is a perfect example of physical Bitcoins being created on a somewhat casual basis by members of the community as more hobby than business. Physical Bitcoin manufacturers generally fall into one of three categories: serious business ventures focused on profit, hobbyists with inspiration for producing an interesting coin design and looking to make a small profit while contributing to the community, and those that are an equal mix of both. Anarcoins is an excellent example of the casual hobbyist, who created something valuable for the community.

Image Credits (clockwise): John Sacco, Anarcoins

Anarcoins

Goxxed For the Last Time Silver

Manufacturer: Anarcoins
Year: 2014
Denomination: BTC
Type: Round

Version	Mintage
Normal	500
Anniversary	3
TOTAL	**503**

Material: .999 Silver
Diameter: 39 mm
Thickness: 2.7 mm
Weight: 1 oz
Country: UK

This is a round to commiserate (not to commemorate) the infamous collapse of the Mt.Gox Bitcoin exchange. In the early days of trading when Mt.Gox was the most popular exchange, users referred to the suffering of trading losses or bitcoin value decreases seemingly caused by the faulty operation of the exchange as being 'Goxxed'. With the failure of the exchange, all those who lost their balances were essentially 'Goxxed' for the last time. The front of the coin features an image of Mark Karpeles (the owner of the exchange) and a BTC price chart showing the rise and fall of BTC value in December 2013.

Image Credits (clockwise): Elias Ahonen, Anarcoins

Anarcoins

Goxxed For the Last Time Plated

Manufacturer: Anarcoins
Year: 2014, 2015
Denomination: BTC
Type: Round

Version	Mintage
Normal Pl.	500
Anniversary Silver Pl.	80
Anniversary Gold Pl.	80
TOTAL	**660**

Material:
Silver Pl. Copper/Zinc Alloy
Gold Pl. Copper/Zinc Alloy
Diameter: 39 mm
Thickness: 2.7 mm
Weight: 33.2 g
Country: UK

In addition to the imagery, there is a text stating "mt.gox:r.i.p....?" surrounded by question marks along with the date on which the exchange was shut down. The price chart is included in reference to allegations that both the initial rise and crash of BTC value were caused by the Mt.Gox exchange, and the question marks attempt to communicate the aura of confusion that surrounded the exchange's failure, price fluctuations, and Mr. Karpeles. The other side features a 'meme' image of Jean-Luc Picard (a *Star Trek* character) in a frustrated 'face-palm' in reference to the falling value of BTC. The "Don't Get...." refers to a warning of not getting 'Goxxed' again. On the one-year anniversary of the shut-down, a special 'Anniversary edition' was released for both the silver and silver plated coins, along with the addition of a new gold-plated version. These special 'Anniversary' editions are designated by the text 'Commiserative Anniversary Edition' being etched onto the back.

Image Credits (clockwise): Elias Ahonen, Howard Kesselman

Anarcoins

Unobtanium Silver Wallet

Silver Plated Bar, 2014

Manufacturer: Anarcoins
Year: 2014, 2015
Denomination: UNO
Type: DIY

Version	Mintage
2014 Silver Pl. Copper	200
2015 Gold Pl.	29
TOTAL	**229**

Material: Silver Pl. Copper
Diameter: 50 x 30 mm
Thickness: 3 mm
Weight: 39.5 g
Country: UK

The Unobtanium Bar (Silver Wallet, as it is called by Anarcoins) is themed after a crypto-currency called Unobtanium. Although it is struck with the words '.999 Fine Silver', only half (numbers 1-50 and 100-150) of the bars are actually pure silver whereas the other half (numbers 51-99 and 151-200) are silver plated copper. The bars also contain the words 'Rare, Resilient, Secure', and come with a security hologram which the buyer can use to secure their own crypto-currency in a DIY fashion. Of the silver plated bars, 25 have been gold plated, and another 4 are gold plated errors.

Silver Bar, 2014

Manuf.	Anarcoins
Year	2014
Denom.	UNO
Type	DIY
Mintage	200
Material	.999 Silver
Diameter	50 x 30 mm
Thickness	3 mm
Weight	47 g
Country	UK

Image Credits (clockwise): Howard Kesselman (all)

Anonymous Mint

Guardian

Manuf.	Anonymous Mint
Year	
Denom.	BTC
Type	Round
Mintage	
Material	.999 Copper
Diameter	
Thickness	
Weight	1 oz
Country	USA

This copper round is the first in a series of three produced by Anonymous Mint. The coin features an image of 'The Guardian', "a symbolic representation of those who are keeping an eye on the ruling elite that keep an eye on *us*". The coin is very similar to and likely inspired by the 'Series 1.0 Satoshi' coin produced by Ravenbit, and it would be fair to interpret the 'Guardian' as being Satoshi. Behind the 'digitized' outline of a man, a gear shape is apparent, symbolizing the automated technology on which Bitcoin is based. The front features the text 'Anonymous Mint – 1 oz AVDP – .999 Copper'. The 'AVDP' refers to the 'avoirdupois system', which is simply a name for the system of weights upon which ounces and pounds are based. The back has a Bitcoin 'B' super-imposed on a background of binary 1's and 0's, similarly to earlier coins such as those released by MJB Monetary Metals. The text 'Premier Peer To Peer Crypto Currency – Physical Artifact For The Real World' is written around the outer edge. This text clearly explains the purpose of the coin; an 'artifact' of Bitcoin so that the digital concept can be more easily understood.

Image Credits (clockwise): Copperhead Bullion, Elias Ahonen

Anonymous Mint

Silk Road

Manuf.	Anonymous Mint
Year	
Denom.	BTC
Type	Round
Mintage	
Material	.999 Copper
Diameter	
Thickness	
Weight	1 oz
Country	USA

These copper rounds depict the logo of 'The Silk Road', which was an online marketplace on the so-called 'Dark Web' accessible only via the specialized 'Tor' browser. The marketplace exclusively used BTC as the medium of exchange. Anyone could create an account to buy or sell anything anonymously, leading to an almost unimaginable offering of illegal drugs, fake identification documents, counterfeit money, and various 'hacking' services. The Silk Road gained some notoriety in the media as a hub of internet 'lawlessness'. Launched in 2011, The Silk Road was perhaps the first practical indication of Bitcoin being a viable economic system, with price fluctuations having little effect on the transactions taking place. Due to its use on The Silk Road, Bitcoin's early reputation of being linked to drugs and other criminal activities was influential in the media. The website was shut down by the FBI in October 2013, and Ross Ulbricht was sentenced to life in prison due to his involvement in creating and running it. Over 144,000 BTC was seized from Ulbricht's computer, which was later sold in a series of auctions by the U.S. Marshals Service. This sale by the U.S. government was seen as an important indicator of Bitcoin's legitimacy and acceptance government.

Image Credits (clockwise): Elias Ahonen (all)

Anonymous Mint

Anonymous

Manuf.	Anonymous Mint
Year	
Denom.	BTC
Type	Round
Mintage	
Material	.999 Copper
Diameter	
Thickness	
Weight	1 oz
Country	USA

This third and final round in the series features a representation of the 'Anonymous' logo. Anonymous is an infamous Internet 'organization' loosely composed of various activist groups and hackers, some of them colloquially known as 'hacktivists'. The organization is based on the idea of anonymity, and anyone can essentially become 'Anonymous' by participating in its actions. With no leadership structure, Anonymous is de-centralized and operates on a peer-to-peer bases in the same way as Bitcoin. In addition to this similarity, both are associated with concepts of online anonymity (or more accuratly, pseudonomy), and even actions such as hacking. Due to these similarities and the fact that they have been in the public radar at approximately the same time, some have erroneously associated Anonymous directly with Bitcoin. While it is likely that some Anonymous participants are Bitcoin users, there is no real connection between the two, as evidenced by the fact that the Wikipedia page for Anonymous does not even mention Bitcoin (at the time of writing). As such, the 'Anonymous' design has no real relevance to Bitcoin, though many will recognize it along with Bitcoin as a 'force' that cannot be ignored in the current digital realm.

Image Credits (clockwise): Copperhead Bullion, Elias Ahonen

Antana

Antana was created by Anton and Ana of Melbourne, Australia. The name is a combination of the creator's names. The idea behind Antana's coins is unique, in that they mark 'difficulty changes' in the Bitcoin network which happen approximately every ten days. The back of each coin contains a date, and 'network statistics' from that day are recorded on the coin. In addition to recording something news-worthy going on in the crypto-currency sphere at the time, four metrics are recorded for perpetuity: hash rate, difficulty, block, and total BTC. They are explained below:

Hash Rate refers to the processing power of the Bitcoin network, calculated in 'Thash/s' (1 Thash/s or Th/s is equivalent to one trillion calculations per second).

Difficulty refers to the relative maximum amount of processing power that is needed to find the next block.

Block refers to a 'confirmation' on the network which settles transactions. New blocks are created at approximately 10 minute intervals. The number on the coin refers to the block that was reached that day.

Total BTC refers to the total amount of Bitcoin that has been mined into existence from Bitcoin's launch to the date on the coin.

Since all Antana coins are identical in composition, size, and weight, they are all recorded in a single table. A total of 21 coins have been released, perhaps to intentionally refer to 21 million bitcoins which is the maximum amount of BTC that can ever exist.

Manufacturer: Antana
Year: 2013, 2014
Denomination: BTC
Type: Round

Version	Year	Mintage
#124	2013	300
#125	2013	300
#126	2013	300
#127	2013	300
#128	2013	300
#129	2013	300
#130	2013	300
#131	2013	300
#132	2013	300
#133	2013	300
#134	2013	300
#135	2013	300
#136	2013	300
#137	2014	300
#138	2014	300
#139	2014	300
#140	2014	300
#141	2014	300
#142	2014	300
#143	2014	300
#144	2014	300
TOTAL		6,300

Material: Gold Pl. Zinc
Diameter: 40 mm
Thickness: 3 mm
Weight: 1 oz
Country: Australia

Image Credits: Antana (all)

Antana

#124 Satoshi Nakamoto (03-08-2013)

The first Antana coin celebrates the creator of Bitcoin. It is dated 03-08-2013, when 11.49 million BTC existed and the Hash Rate was 294 Terahashes per second.

#125 ASICMiner USB Block Erupter (13-04-2013)

ASICMiner's Block Erupters were USB-stick sized 'mining rigs' that could be plugged into any USB port to immediately start earning BTC in a very efficient manner.

Image Credits (clockwise): Antana (all)

Antana

#126 God Save The Mt.Gox (24-08-2013)

At the time this coin was released, Mt. Gox was the dominant Bitcoin exchange and despite its many faults, was a backbone of the Bitcoin economy.

#127 "Regulations? Try me" (04-09-2013)

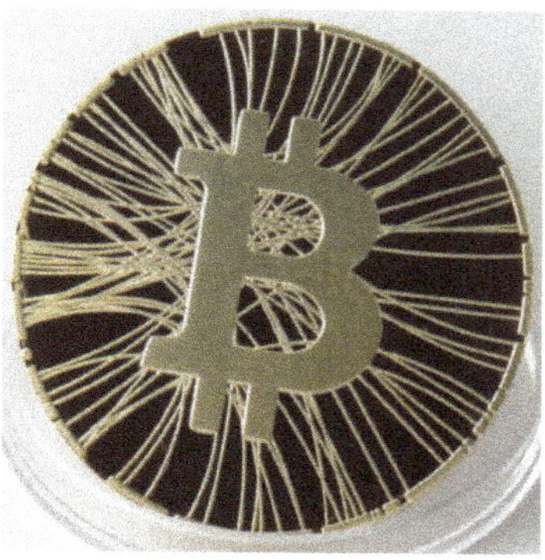

The statement on this coin is in reference to discussions regarding the possibly unavoidable future regulation of crypto-currency. The coin is conveying the message that crypto-currency cannot be regulated even if authorities attempt to do so.

#128 "Mining on my own" (15-09-2013)

This coin refers to 'solo mining' which is when no 'mining pool' is used to evenly distribute earnings. A solo miner keep all the BTC they uncover, but it can be risky as they can also go for extended periods without any earnings.

Image Credits (clockwise): Antana (all)

Antana

#129 "Just Type Bitcoin" (25-09-2013)

This quote was posted on the website Reddit by someone who was told to simply 'type Bitcoin' into a Bloomberg financial news terminal in order to find relevant information. The suggestion is that Bitcoin is becoming recognized in the financial sector.

#130 "Bitcointalk hacked" (06-10-2013)

Bitcointalk.org, a key discussion forum for Bitcoin developers and influencers was hacked and temporarily disabled by a group of hackers calling themselves 'The Hole Seekers'.

#131 "Baidu Is In" (16-10-2013)

China's largest search engine, Baidu, began accepting BTC as payment for firewall and DDoS security products.

Image Credits (clockwise): Antana (all)

Antana

#132 "TO THE MOON | TO THE EARTH" (26-10-2013)

'TO THE MOON' is a humorous saying amongst some bitcoin holders and traders, referring to their belief that Bitcoin price will skyrocket. It is often seen in commentary during times of price increase. The opposite 'To The Earth' is true when the price is declining.

#133 "First Bitcoin ATM" (05-11-2013)

The first bitcoin ATM was installed in Vancouver, Canada. They generally work both ways, allowing anyone to insert cash and receive BTC, or conveniently sell their BTC for cash. Hundreds of Bitcoin ATM's have since been installed worldwide.

#134 "500 USD | 3000 CNY | 50000 JPY" (17-11-2013)

In November 2013, Bitcoin reached milestone values in three national currencies. These three countries have a significant portion of the world's Bitcoin users. Hash Rate is at 5,000 Th/s, up from only 294 in March.

Image Credits (clockwise): Antana (all)

Antana

#135 "Pump And Dump" (30-11-2013)

New crypto-currencies are often subject to 'Pump and Dump' schemes: hype is created to rapidly increase the price so that the organizers can sell their holdings for huge profits.

#136 "Thank You Casascius" (01-12-2013)

Casascius is widely acknowledged as having jump-started the physical crypto-currency phenomenon. Due to FinCEN requests, he stopped most sales.

Image Credits (clockwise): Antana (all)

Antana

#137 "Race For ROI" (22-12-2013)

At this point, mining is becoming increasingly competitive and profit margins are decreasing. For a new entrant without the means for very large infrastructure and cheap electricity, just breaking even can be a challenge.

#138 "5,317 %" (02-01-2014)

5,317 percent. That is the amount that BTC rose in 2013. Lots of people made large amounts of money, and a significant amount of public interest was generated. 12.2 million bitcoins exist at this point.

#139 "AntMiner" (12-01-2014)

The 'AntMiner' is launched, putting significant processing power of up to two Gh/s per unit into the hands of anyone looking to invest a few hundred dollars. Small mining operations became profitable again.

Image Credits (clockwise): Antana (all)

Antana

#140 "Believe In Altcoins" (24-01-2014)

Hundreds of 'alt coins' on the market, competing with Bitcoin and each other. While they are extremely volatile and often suffer from a lack of accountability, some show evidence of real innovation and opportunity.

#141 "Bitcoin VS. Apple" (05-02-2014)

When Apple Inc. banned Bitcoin wallets from the app store, their products could no longer be used in Bitcoin transactions.

#142 "Transaction Malleability" (17-02-2014)

Transaction malleability refers to an issue with the Bitcoin network. It makes it possible for a payment to appear valid, but on a basis of invalid data. Only when a new block is formed is a transaction confirmed to be final.

Image Credits (clockwise): Antana (all)

Antana

#143 "Goodbye, MT.GOX" (17-02-2014)

After a long history of problems, the exchange Mt.Gox shut down, leaving users without the ability to access $450,000,000 worth of their BTC.

#144 "I am not Dorian Nakamoto" (13-03-2014)

A Newsweek reporter wrote an expose claiming to have identified a Japanese-American named Dorian Nakamoto as Satoshi. A presumed hacker then used Satoshi Nakamoto's profile on the P2P Foundation to declare that he was not Dorian.

Image Credits (clockwise): Antana (all)

Antaui

Silver WorldCoin

Manuf.	Antaui
Year	2013
Denom.	5 WDC
Type	PF
Mintage	500
Material	.999 Silver
Diameter	39 mm
Thickness	3 mm
Weight	1 ozt
Country	

Antaui was created by Nathan Gudmunson, a PHP developer who was head of development (and chair of the board) for Worldcoin. Worldcoin is an alternative crypto-currency which once had a very active community base and a market cap peak of nearly 24 million USD in late 2013. These coins were produced at the time of Worldcoin's peak value, which has fallen from about 90 cents (USD) to less 1 percent of that.

Like many alternative crypto-currencies, Worldcoin was an attempt to innovate on Bitcoin to successfully launch a new, stable, and global monetary system. While most attempts at such a lofty goal are likely to be unsuccessful, the innovations that are taking place are no doubt setting the stage for something even better in the future. Coins like this are perhaps the only lasting physical evidence of the long process of technological and social progress which may one day transform the world and society we live in with a new concept of money and all its unknown consequences.

The front features the Worldcoin logo along with '5 WDC', with which it is pre-funded. The backside has a custom hologram covering the entire surface.

Image Credits (clockwise): Howard Kesselman (all)

AussieBTC

Loadable Casascius Aluminum Bitcoin

Manuf.	AussieBTC
Year	2014
Denom.	BTC
Type	UF, DIY
Mintage	
Material	Aluminum
Diameter	32 mm
Thickness	1.3 mm
Weight	2.7 g
Country	Australia

AussieBTC is created with the same idea as Cryptofreeze and its inspiration, Serpcoin. The coins are made with Casascius aluminum DIY coins, with a custom hologram on which the entire public key is printed. Like Cryptofreeze, the coins are unfunded. While coins like this are quite easy to make and additional 'brands' made with Casascius DIY coins are not likely to be notable in the future development of physical crypto-currencies, the first instances of such coins are worth mentioning due to their early introduction in 2013 and 2014. After acquiring a number of these coins, TGBEX began to offer them as 'free gifts' with all orders.

Image Credits (clockwise): Howard Kesselman (all)

Banx Mint

1 BTC

Manuf.	Banx Mint
Year	2015
Denom.	1, 5, 10 BTC
Type	PF
Mintage	
Material	Gold Pl. Alloy
Diameter	38 mm
Thickness	4 mm
Weight	22 g
Country	UK

This coin design has the Bitcoin 'B' and the Litecoin 'L' superimposed onto a 'circuit board' background, symbolizing the technological basis of crypto-currency. This design is directly inspired by MJB Monetary Metal's original circuit board design, which is displayed on the photo to the right. Additional coins have been made in 5 BTC, 10 BTC, 5 LTC, and 10 LTC denominations. Their designs are identical, except for the denomination on the front.

1 LTC

Manuf.	Banx Mint
Year	2015
Denom.	1, 5, 10 LTC
Type	PF
Mintage	
Material	Silver Pl. Alloy
Diameter	38 mm
Thickness	4 mm
Weight	22 g
Country	UK

Banx Mint is one of eleven subsidiaries of Banx Capital. The other businesses include a crypto-currency exchange, crypto-currency scratch cards, currency exchange, remittances, and crowd-funding. The company is primarily owned by Mark Lyford, who has organized sales of 'Banx Shares' on the Bitcointalk forum.

Image Credits (clockwise): Howard Kesselman (4)

bhCoin

bhCoin was among the early entrants to the physical Bitcoin market. Based in Argentina and minted in China, the company has released seven different coins to date.

"This type of storage medium is more reliable than CD/DVD, memory stick or hard drives, as technologies became obsolete [more] quickly than metal coins. You can keep a piece of history that can be transferred to your sons, grandsons as future value increases."[1]

Their location in Argentina, which has highly protectionist political policies, has been a challenge due to strict importing and exporting rules. bhcoin has nevertheless been successful, and due to their early entrance to the market and limited production they may well reach their stated goal of producing coins which will hold historical significance. bhcoin has announced plans to release an open source version of their 'offline wallet generator', which would be freely available to anyone loading their own physical Bitcoins.

Image Credits (clockwise): bhcoin (all)

1. bhCoin source unaccessible

bhCoin

Series 1

Manuf.	bhCoin
Year	2013
Denom.	0.1 BTC
Type	PF
Mintage	100
Material	Gold Pl. Brass
Diameter	26 mm
Thickness	2.15 mm
Weight	8 g
Country	Argentina

Being denominated in the curious 'bitCents', they were designed when Bitcoin was still of a relatively low value, as the term is no longer in use for the amount. The coins contain a private key and QR code within a square pit in the middle. They are numbered 1-100.

These coins break from the trend set by Casascius and feature an simple but original front instead of a prominent Bitcoin symbol. Considered a prototype by its creators, it was meant to be cheap, having a lower denomination compared to the available Casascius coins at the time.

A significant issue came about regarding shipping, as it reportedly cost up to ten times the cost of a single coin to have said coin shipped from Argentina.

Image Credits (clockwise): Howard Kesselman (all)

bhCoin

Series 2

Manuf.	bhCoin
Year	2013
Denom.	0.1 BTC
Type	PF
Mintage	100
Material	Silver Pl.
Diameter	28 mm
Thickness	2 mm
Weight	11.1 g
Country	Argentina

Released two months after V1, this coin holds a more traditional front design, with "bhCoin 2013, Vires In Numeris, 10 bitCents" written in a separate groove at the edge. The hologram is a silver version of V1.

It is notable that these coins do not begin again at serial number 1, but continue where V1 left off, 101-200.

Image Credits (clockwise): Elias Ahonen (all)

bhCoin

2F Series 3

Manuf.	bhCoin
Year	2013
Denom.	0.1 BTC
Type	UF
Mintage	200
Material	Silver Pl.
Diameter	28 mm
Thickness	2 mm
Weight	9.4 g
Country	Argentina

This coin is designated as a '2-factor' coin, because it requires more than the hidden private key to release contained funds. Each coin was shipped with a certificate containing a code for the specific coin, which is needed along with the private key to release any contained funds. These coins did not come pre-funded, and range from serial numbers 203 to 403. If the number on the certificate is lost, no BTC can be redeemed from the coin.

Image Credits (clockwise): Elias Ahonen (all)

bhCoin

Series 4 DIY physical bitcoin (Antique Golden)

Manuf.	bhCoin
Year	2015
Denom.	BTC
Type	UF, DIY
Mintage	150
Material	Ant. Gold
Diameter	28 mm
Thickness	2 mm
Weight	8.6 g
Country	Argentina

This series of 600 coins is divided into four different metallic finishes, with 150 of each type made. They were shipped either as unfunded or DIY, according to the customer's wishes. Though creating four finishes instead of one is naturally more expensive, it was done with the intention of creating variety and encouraging collectors to buy one of each. The antique gold coin was sold out first, indicating its desirability to buyers. Compared to most coins, these have a large amount of clear space. The Bitcoin 'B' is also both on an angle and partly concealed, which is very unusual.

Image Credits (clockwise): Elias Ahonen (all)

bhCoin

Series 4 DIY physical bitcoin (Mirror Golden)

Manuf.	bhCoin
Year	2015
Denom.	BTC
Type	UF, DIY
Mintage	150
Material	Gold Pl.
Diameter	28 mm
Thickness	2 mm
Weight	8.6 g
Country	Argentina

Series 4 DIY physical bitcoin (Mirror Silver)

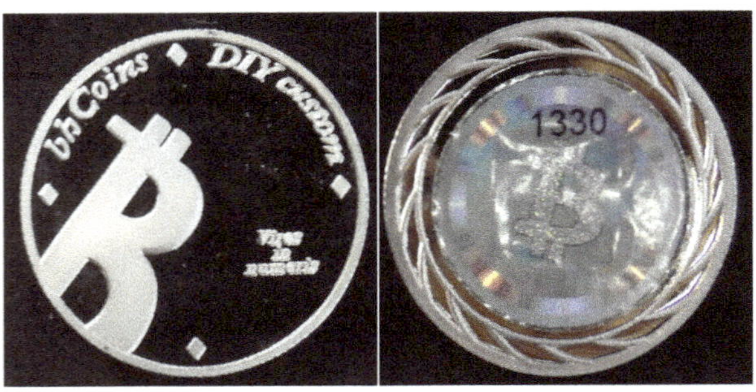

Manuf.	bhCoin
Year	2015
Denom.	BTC
Type	UF, DIY
Mintage	150
Material	Silver Pl.
Diameter	28 mm
Thickness	2 mm
Weight	8.6 g
Country	Argentina

Series 4 DIY physical bitcoin (Antique Silver)

Manuf.	bhCoin
Year	2015
Denom.	BTC
Type	UF, DIY
Mintage	150
Material	Ant. Silver
Diameter	28 mm
Thickness	2 mm
Weight	8.6 g
Country	Argentina

Image Credits (clockwise): Elias Ahonen (all)

Image Credits (clockwise): Bitcoin Nerd (all)

Bitcoin Nerd

(and The Bitcoin Museum)

'The Bitcoin Museum' is an online museum run by Andrew Dobbins, an early collector of bitcoin memorabilia and notably physical Bitcoins. Though he purchased many items himself, The Bitcoin Museum has also received many donations from the creators of physical coins and other Bitcoin items.

Inspired by the 1 gram silver rounds made by MJB Monetary Metals, he created two small silver coins to commemorate important days in the history of Bitcoin, using 'Bitcoin Nerd' as a personal brand. Though the first series sold well, the second version had difficulty selling out the full 1,000 mintage.

In June 2014, Andrew's computer was hacked where 14 BTC was stolen, which included all proceeds from his sales of Bitcoin Nerd items. Because the funds were about to be used to pay for an upcoming wedding and honeymoon, the loss amounted to a personal tragedy. Without other avenues to pay the remaining costs, he appealed to the Bitcointalk.org community for help, and initiated an auction of all physical Bitcoins and memorabilia that he owned and not been donated to him. Since this auction had numerous rare coins that are rarely offered for sale, it generated great interest amongst collectors. Close to the end of the auction, a member of the community offered Andrew an interest-free 10 BTC loan. This was sufficient to cancel the desperate auction, and many other members of the forum offered loans and even donations which were enough to cover the entire loss. As promised, Mr. Dobbins repaid all loans in full. Though the bitcoin community can often be harsh, this has been a wonderful example of many individuals coming together to help someone who has long been involved with Bitcoin and contributed to the community.

Left: the 'Bitcoin Nerd' (top), v2 silver rounds (bottom)

Bitcoin Nerd

The Genesis Block

Manuf.	Bitcoin Nerd
Year	2013
Denom.	BTC
Type	Round
Mintage	1,000
Material	.999 Silver
Diameter	15 mm
Thickness	0.75 mm
Weight	1 g
Country	Australia

Created as a fundraiser for 'The Bitcoin Museum', this coin commemorates the 'Genesis Block'; the first block of Bitcoin mined by Satoshi on January 3rd, 2009.

The reverse displays the historic address to which the genesis block was mined, and where it still remains today. Interestingly, some additional BTC has been sent to the address as a 'gift' to Satoshi.

Image Credits (clockwise): Elias Ahonen (all)

Bitcoin Nerd

The 10,000 Bitcoin Pizza

Manuf.	Bitcoin Nerd
Year	2013
Denom.	BTC
Type	Round
Mintage	1,000
Material	.999 Silver
Diameter	15 mm
Thickness	0.75 mm
Weight	1 g
Country	Australia

Launched after a successful sale of the 'Genesis Block' coins, the 'Bitcoin Pizza' coin memorializes another day in Bitcoin history. On May 22nd, 2010 (16th month of BTC existence), the first ever purchase using bitcoin was made. Laszlo Hanyecz traded 10,000 BTC which he had mined for two pizzas, which the 'buyer' of the BTC placed an order to have delivered to his door. This transaction was incredibly significant, because it was the first time that BTC was demonstrated to have real-world value. The bitcoin address on the back is that into which the BTC was sent.

Image Credits (clockwise): Elias Ahonen (all)

Bitcoin Penny

Bitcoin Penny launched in March 2015, bringing something fresh to the collectible Bitcoin scene. It is identical to the standard US 1 cent coin in color and proportions, but instead has a bitcoin theme. It joins a long tradition of 'novelty coins' that have been made for many decades in the likeness of coins between 1 and 25 cents in value.

"ONCE UPON A TIME, an American bitcoin enthusiast and lover of fine leather shoes was sitting at his office desk when he glanced down at his favorite penny loafers. In a moment of playful inspiration, he thought, 'People have been wearing the same old pennies in their penny loafers for decades. It's a fun and fashionable tradition, but isn't it time we update that tradition for the twenty-first century? We use digital currency now. We need a digital penny. We need a… BITCOIN PENNY!'"[1]

Judging by the name, it is fair to assume that the venture will not diversify much, perhaps releasing a new design once the initial stock is sold.

Below: Traditional Penny Loafers with the Bitcoin Penny (left), a roll of 40 Bitcoin Penny rounds, (upper right), 'Penny Loafer' key-chain sold by Bitcoin Penny (lower right)

Image Credits (clockwise): Bitcoin Penny (all)

1. "The Bitcoin Penny Story" Link: http://thebitcoinpenny.com/pages/the-bitcoin-penny-story

The Bitcoin Penny Company

Bitcoin Penny Commemorative Coin

Manuf.	Bitcoin Penny
Year	2015
Denom.	BTC
Type	Round
Mintage	
Material	Copper
Diameter	23 mm
Thickness	2 mm
Weight	6 g
Country	USA

This bitcoin 'penny' is a play on the real US 1 cent coin, being of similar size and material. The round proclaims 'In Code We Trust', in contrast with the 'In God We Trust' declaration on US currency. The meaning of this can be taken further, to symbolize how digital currencies operate on real objective mathematic principles (code) as opposed to the control of a 'higher power' such as a government or central bank (God). Furthermore, 'E Pluribus Unum' is replaced with 'E-Currency Unum'. Notably, the 'B' on this coin is a different font than usual on physical Bitcoins.

Image Credits (clockwise): Elias Ahonen (all)

BTC Trinkets

Challenge Coin - Bitcoin One

Manuf.	BTC Trinkets
Year	2013
Denom.	1 BTC
Type	Round
Mintage	
Material	
Diameter	45 mm
Thickness	5 mm
Weight	49 g
Country	Finland

BTC Trinkets – Bitcoin Niche Items is an online store based in Finland and run by Eero Tulppala. The store sells various items, including bitcoin themed pins, pens, leather wallets, clothes, and key-chains. These two 'challenge coins' are amongst products produced and sold by Tulppala. Challenge coins carry the name because they often, though not always,, celebrate some achievement. They have a long history, and are often produced in fairly small batches to give event participants for commemorative purposes, for example in the militaries of various countries. These coins simply commemorate Bitcoin.

Challenge Coin - Bitcoin Five

Manuf.	BTC Trinkets
Year	2013
Denom.	5 BTC
Type	Round
Mintage	
Material	
Diameter	45 mm
Thickness	5 mm
Weight	49 g
Country	Finland

These rounds have no year of manufacture or other markings, and are simply meant to represent Bitcoin. The design on the 'One' coin represents the Bitcoin network and is an early example of the 'network' design used by Ravenbit and Coinographic. The 'Five' coin design symbolizes the blockchain, with five 'blocks' connected by a chain. These rounds are amongst the largest crypto-currency themed physical coins ever made.

Image Credits (clockwise): BTC Trinkets (all)

Casascius Physical Bitcoins

Mike Caldwell first learned about Bitcoin in late 2010, and became very interested in its technical aspects. Being a programmer, he was able to understand the abstract technical principles behind Bitcoin but had difficulty simplifying the concept into something that could easily be explained to less technically adept people.

The problem was that people had an emotional connection to money as something that could be 'owned', so the concept of 'bits' on the Internet holding monetary value, was too abstract for the average person to understand or remain interested in. For this reason, a bridge needed to be built between computer science and the physical realm. If a bitcoin could be handed to someone, giving them immediate and exclusive ownership of the 'funny-money', then perhaps the concept wouldn't seem quite as crazy. A physical Bitcoin; now that's a conversation starter.

Above: A washer like this with two holograms could have been the first Casascius coin.

Mr. Caldwell came up with the idea of buying a few hundred small metal washers and placing tamper-proof holograms on each side to secure a private key inside. He only considered the idea of minting metal coins after the realization that custom made holograms were expensive and it would actually be cheaper to use a coin and hologram as opposed to two holograms. After some shopping around, he settled on a company that specialized in minting currency for so-called micro-nations in addition to arcade and car-wash tokens. Though physical appearance was not a priority, a Bitcoin themed design was created and soon the first Casascius brass coins were minted. Having no experience in hologram technology, Caldwell deferred to experts who helped to design the series 1 hologram with various security features.

Caldwell had no desire to generate profit with the Casascius venture. Holograms were his greatest initial expense, and the brass tokens cost between 25 and 50 cents each. He ran the business purely as a hobby, funding coins on an ad-hoc basis according to orders, which he accepted only in BTC and priced to merely cover his material expenses. As interest in

Image Credits: Casascius, public domain

Casascius coins increased, improved holograms and a greater range of coins and even bars were released. Early adopters bought large denomination products in multiples, including 1,000 BTC gold coins.

As the value of BTC increased exponentially, Casascius produced smaller denominations of 0.5 BTC and 0.1 BTC. At the same time, buyers became increasingly interested in silver coins even though their production cost and therefore overhead were much higher than for the simple brass coins. These 'luxury' coins became sought after because the value of the BTC they contained was now much greater, and in some ways the use of silver was seen to be more superior to the 'no frills' features of brass coins.

Mr. Caldwell was very aware of the inherent contradiction of trust-less money being stored in a way that allowed a third party (himself) to handle the private keys of others' BTC. By virtue of selling Casascius coins, he felt that he was promoting the idea that he should be trusted with private keys because of his honesty and transparency. He did not want to be trusted in this way, as it violated what he regarded as the true ethos and purpose of bitcoin. In response to this, he invented Bitcoin Improvement Proposal 38, or BIP38 for short. This was a system that allowed Bitcoin to be held in addresses that required a password-protected private key to access. Once the improvement was implemented, Casascius began to promote a new line of 2-factor products that allowed owners to control the private key and ensured that Casascius could not access the funds.

As the value of bitcoin rose significantly, safety became a source of some concern. While the value of BTC that he loaded into the first coins was small at the time, towards the end of his operations he had funded coins with a total of over 90,000 BTC. Had this all been un-redeemed, it would have been worth over 100 million USD during the BTC bubble in late 2013. While he had no way of accessing any of that BTC, someone with bad motives could well assume otherwise.

Contrary to popular belief, FinCEN did not 'shut down' his operations. The federal authorities wanted Mr. Caldwell to register Casascius as a Money Services Business. With the aforementioned issues pressing against him, Caldwell considered the FinCEN involvement as the last straw of complicating factors, and decided not to continue. It is important to remember that Casascius was operating for the purpose of profit, and the compliance with regulatory matters would have been substantially costly.

Casascius could be seen as a victim of its own success, with Caldwell deciding to remove himself from the spotlight in late 2013. Since ending operations, he has moved on to other pursuits and is far less actively involved with Bitcoin. When he first considered the idea of physical Bitcoins, he thought that Bitcoin would make a "funny story someday". It is certain that while many such 'funny stories' make up the history of Bitcoin, the innovation in financial technology that it represents will remain significant even if the currency is surpassed by something superior.

All things considered, Mr. Caldwell is and will remain the father of the physical crypto-currency phenomena, and has inspired hundreds of different coins and rounds into existence.

Counterfeiting Incident

Casascius coins are selling for increasingly high amounts, and with such amounts changing hands it is only a matter of time before fake products enter the market. Few things of value are immune to this; there is fake money, fake bullion bars, fake passports and fake versions of nearly every perfume and clothing brand. Counterfeiting cannot be stopped, but steps can be taken to avoid buying an un-original product. To date, there has only been one known case of a fake coin being listed for sale; a 'convincing' 25 BTC coin was listed on eBay by new user 'tradus 1980' in February 2014. Two months prior, a photo showing a sheet of hologram stickers mimicking Casascius' series 1 1 BTC 2011 coins came to light, with each sticker having a unique code. They are similar but clearly identifiable to the trained eye; they have not appeared for sale to date (it cannot be confirmed if the fake on eBay used one of these). Casascius commented on the incident, saying that "They use a different type face for the main Casascius as well as a slightly different B-logo shape. My series 1 coins also use a dot-matrix style printing with fixed width characters, rather than the solid characters in a proportional font that appear in this photo."[1]

Above: two of the unauthorized holograms on their wax sheet.

Assuming that Casascius coins (and other physical crypto-currencies) increase in value and maintain a robust market, it is likely that increasingly convincing replications will be passed on as original coins bearing a crypto-currency balance. The best defense against such actions is education and information, as well as a healthy suspicion and attentiveness.

Image Credits: Unknown, Casascius

1. "POSSIBLE COUNTERFEITS TO BE AWARE OF" Link: https://casascius.wordpress.com/2013/12/10/possible-counterfeits-to-be-aware-of/

Casascius Physical Bitcoin

Series 1 1 BTC 2011 'Error'

Manufacturer: Casascius
Year: 2011
Denomination: 1 BTC
Type: PF

Load Year	Total	Unopened
2011	4,160	3,419
2012	1,578	1,390
2013	371	371
2014		
Total	**6,109**	**5,180**

Material: Brass
Diameter: 28.5 mm
Thickness: 1.5 mm
Weight: 6.8 g
Country: USA
Best Grade: MS-69

Announced on September 6th of 2011, these coins were the first funded physical Bitcoins ever produced.

They are sought after both for their significance as the first coin of their type, but also due to the added perception of rarity due to a spelling error (Casascius is spelled as 'CASACIUS') in the small hologram text.

There are two special varieties of this coin. For one, 1,574 of these were actually funded in early 2012. Second, there is an ultra-rare type in which the first-bits are not in the middle, but significantly higher on the hologram. Only five of these exist.

In December of 2013, an image of fake holograms imitating the error emerged. This was the first counterfeiting related incident regarding physical crypto-currency.

Image Credits (clockwise): Andrew Dobbins (all)

Casascius Physical Bitcoin

Series 1 1 BTC 2011 'Double Error'

Manufacturer: Casascius
Year: 2011
Denomination: 1 BTC
Type: PF

Load Year	Total	Unopened
2011		
2012	5*	?
2013		
2014		
Total	**5***	**?**

Material: Brass
Diameter: 28.5 mm
Thickness: 1.5 mm
Weight: 6.8 g
Country: USA

These five coins are distinctive in having the first-bits, which are usually in the middle of the hologram, printed 3 mm higher than normal.

The specific coins and even load year are unknown, but they are all series 1 1 BTC 2011 'Error' coins, making these five the rarest of the already sought-after variety.

Overlooking the prototype gold coin, this is the rarest Casascius coin. At the time of writing, only one has been 'discovered'. Considering that about a fifth of the series 1 1 BTC 2011 coins have been redeemed, it is probable that not all five remain unredeemed . Of any that have been redeemed, it is very unlikely that the peeled hologram(s) will ever surface as they were not considered worth preserving. Considering also that many early Casascius coins were given as gifts and forgotten, it remains to be seen if more of these coins surface with time.

*These numbers are not subtracted from the series 1 1 BTC 2011stats.

Image Credits (clockwise): Andrew Dobbins, Morris La Mantia

Casascius Physical Bitcoin

Series 1 1 BTC 2011 'Demo Coin'

Manuf.	Casascius
Year	2011
Denom.	1 BTC
Type	UF
Mintage	
Material	Brass
Diameter	28.5 mm
Thickness	1.5 mm
Weight	6.8 g
Country	USA

Image Credits (clockwise): Scott Barnett

These are the first experimental coins made by Casascius. They were used to test the holograms to reveal the honeycomb pattern left behind, without ever being funded.

The coins can be identified by looking up the public key on a peeled, seemingly 'pre-funded' coin. If no BTC has ever been in the address, then it is possibly a demo coin. Currently, demo coins are only known to exist in brass 1 BTC form.

Casascius sold these coins to prior buyers as extras. On a few occasions, buyers who ordered Casascius coins had the option to also buy some 'demo' coins along with them.

While no numbers relating to these coins exist, it is no doubt that they are extremely rare compared to the mintages of normal Casascius coins. It has been suggested that these coins may be an effective way to invest in the collectable value of Casascius coins without exposure to BTC price fluctuations.

Casascius Physical Bitcoin

Series 2 1 BTC 2011

Manufacturer: Casascius
Year: 2011
Denomination: 1 BTC
Type: PF

Load Year	Total	Unopened
2011	1,644*	1,400*
2012		
2013		
2014		
Total	**1,644***	**1,400***

Material: Brass
Diameter: 28.5 mm
Thickness: 1.5 mm
Weight: 6.8 g
Country: USA
Best Grade: MS-66

Appearing only two months after the Series 1 coins, Series 2 was a significant innovation. This new version utilizes a hologram with a small window to prove the presence of the first-bits and private key inside, making it impossible to rub the first-bits off and fraudulently print a new public key onto the hologram. It is worth taking note that these coins are in fact much more rare then the Series 1 1 BTC 'Error Coin'.

*Numbers refer to series 2 1 BTC 2011 coins funded in 2011. There may be a small additional number that were funded in 2012 and are counted in the series 2 1 BTC 2012 numbers.

Below: a close-up of the center section of the hologram

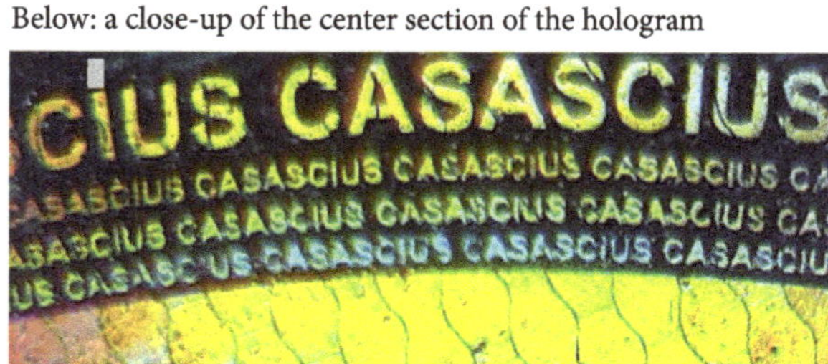

Image Credits (clockwise): Andrew Dobbins, Jon Allen

Casascius Physical Bitcoin

Series 2 1 BTC 2012

Manufacturer: Casascius
Year: 2012
Denomination: 1 BTC
Type: PF

Load Year	Total	Unopened
2011		
2012	4,089*	3,501*
2013		
2014		
Total	**4,089***	**3,501***

Material: Brass
Diameter: 28.5 mm
Thickness: 1.5 mm
Weight: 6.8 g
Country: USA
Best Grade: MS-69

This coin is identical to the 2011 version, except the year '2012' is displayed on the front.

A significant number (nearly a fourth) of these coins have been redeemed, most likely as a direct result of the dramatic rise in Bitcoin value in late 2013.

*The numbers refer to series 2 1 BTC coins funded in 2012. This number may possibly contain a small number of coins marked '2011'.

In August 2013 at DEF CON 21, it was reported that a Casascius coin was successfully compromised. It was done by injecting small amounts of certain chemicals through a small hole in the hologram using a hypodermic needle. This allowed the hologram to be removed and replaced. Reportedly, the hologram of the tampered coin was not as 'vibrant' as non-tampered ones. There have not been any reports of a compromised coin 'in the wild' or being put up for sale.

Image Credits (clockwise): Andrew Dobbins (2), Bitcointalk.org user 'etotheipi'

Casascius Physical Bitcoin

Series 2 1 BTC 2013

Manufacturer: Casascius
Year: 2013
Denomination: 1 BTC
Type: PF

Load Year	Total	Unopened
2011		
2012		
2013	8,221	7,726
2014	131	131
Total	**8,352**	**7,857**

Material: Brass
Diameter: 28.5 mm
Thickness: 1.5 mm
Weight: 6.8 g
Country: USA
Best Grade: MS-69

Image Credits (clockwise): Elias Ahonen (all)

This is the 2013 version of the 1 BTC brass coin. It is the most common Casascius coin when not accounting for the DIY aluminum rounds. 2014 versions of this coin would have surely been even more numerous, had Casascius not ended the sale of pre-funded coins.

This coin was the first to have a 'lobe' cut into the private key pit in order to help stabilize the private key and first-bits during assembly, as they often appeared crooked in older coins.

Some Casascius coins, including up to about 100 1 BTC coins, were funded in 2015 and 2016. They had been originally sold by Casascius to re-sellers during the period of normal operations, who had paid in full with the agreement that funding would happen at a later date when the reseller sold the coins. As far as it is known, all such coins are now funded, with ~36 being in 2015 and ~75 in 2016. It is not known what amount of these late-funded (LF) 1 BTC coins were brass as opposed to silver, but those that were are likely to be this variety.

Casascius Physical Bitcoin

Series 3 1 BTC 2013

Manufacturer: Casascius
Year: 2013
Denomination: 1 BTC
Type: PF

Load Year	Total	Unopened
2011		
2012		
2013	1,300*	*
2014		
Total	**1,300***	*

Material: .999 Silver
Diameter: 39 mm
Thickness: 3 mm
Weight: 1 ozt
Country: USA
Best Grade: MS-70

Notable in this coin is the 'laser rimming' which appears on the edges of the series 3 hologram as a golden texture. Mike theorized that the process would create an interesting obstacle to anyone attempting to tamper with the coins. This process has later been utilized by Lealana for some coins.

These coins were sold and shipped in tubes of 20, though some individual orders were taken initially.

Casascius had originally intended to produce 5 BTC silver coins, but though the mold was created, the plan was scrapped in favor of 1 BTC, 0.5 BTC, and 0.1 BTC series 3 silver coins due to the "tenfold rise in the Bitcoin price over the past four months"[1] to 140 USD.

Interestingly, some of the late-funded (LF) coins were sent to be graded by ANACS long before they were actually funded. That means that ANACS there are a number of slabbed and graded coins which were unfunded at the time that the grading took place.

Image Credits (clockwise): Unknown, Took Groth

1. "REVISED PLANS FOR 2013 SILVER COINS" Link: https://casascius.wordpress.com/2013/04/28/revised-plans-for-2013-silver-coins/

Casascius Physical Bitcoin

Series 3 1 BTC 2013 'Gold Rim'

Manufacturer: Casascius
Year: 2013
Denomination: 1 BTC
Type: PF

Load Year	Total	Unopened
2011		
2012		
2013	700*	*
2014		
Total	**700***	*

Material: .999 Silver
Diameter: 39 mm
Thickness: 3 mm
Weight: 1 ozt
Country: USA
Best Grade: MS-70

This is the same as the original series 3 1 BTC 2013 coin, but with a solid gold plating applied to the 'B' and the outer rim on both sides. This plating is of a higher quality than that of the series 2 10 BTC 2012 'Gold B' coins.

These coins are derived from the series 3 1 BTC 2013 coin of which 2,000* were originally made. 700 of them were converted to this 'Gold Rim' version by Casascius.

*20 of these 2,000 coins have been opened; it is not known what the distribution between normal and 'Gold Rim' is.

Image Credits (clockwise): Jon Allen, Took Groth

Casascius Physical Bitcoin

Series 1 5 BTC 2012 'Error Bitnickel'

Manufacturer: Casascius
Year: 2012
Denomination: 5 BTC
Type: PF, DIY

Load Year	Total	Unopened
2011		
2012	651	570
2013	26	26
2014		
Blanks	N/A	N/A
Total	**677**	**596**

Material: Nickel Pl. Brass
Diameter: 28.5 mm
Thickness: 1.7 mm
Weight: 7.4 g
Country: USA
Best Grade: MS-68

Released in January 2012 with the series 1 hologram, these coins were priced at 6 BTC each. At release, Casascius announced that a silver-tone hologram would be released soon.

All 5 BTC coins appear to have signs of wear on the 'S', 'I', 'N', 'E', 'R,' and 'I' of the 'Vires In Numeris' motto, seemingly created in the minting process.

Casascius later released an unknown number of 40-coin rolls without holograms as blanks, identifying them as 'Roll Your Own'. Such a roll came with sheets of laser cut private key tabs and solid gold colored stickers allowing the buyer to create their own coins by using either the provided private keys or by inserting their own. This sale was likely done due to an excessive stock of Bitnickels.

Image Credits (clockwise): Elias Ahonen, Jon Allen

Casascius Physical Bitcoin

Series 2 5 BTC 2012 'Bitnickel'

Manufacturer: Casascius
Year: 2012
Denomination: 5 BTC
Type: PF

Load Year	Total	Unopened
2011		
2012	133	84
2013	447	367
2014		
Total	**580**	**451**

Material: Nickel Pl. Brass
Diameter: 28.5 mm
Thickness: 1.7 mm
Weight: 7.4 g
Country: USA
Best Grade: MS-68

Released three months after the series 1 'Error Bitnickel' was offered for sale, this is the 'true' Bitnickel featuring a silver (or nickel) tone hologram. Interestingly, less of these were made than the series 1 versions.

On August 18th, 2015, six additional 5 BTC coins were funded by Casascius. These had been fully paid for and delivered years earlier, but funded much later. It is unknown who owns them, but the variety is certainly a unique one.

Image Credits (clockwise): David Bailey, Jon Allen

Casascius Physical Bitcoin

Series 3 0.1 BTC 2013

Manufacturer: Casascius
Year: 2013
Denomination: 0.1 BTC
Type: PF

Load Year	Total	Unopened
2011		
2012	8	7
2013	764	760
2014	37	37
Total	**809**	**804**

Material: .999 Silver
Diameter: 25 mm
Thickness: 1.5 mm (est.)
Weight: 0.25 ozt
Country: USA
Best Grade: MS-70

Image Credits (clockwise): Elias Ahonen (all)

On top of being the smallest denomination Casascius coin, this was also the last. Had Casascius continued the production of coins into later years, it is likely that he would have moved towards smaller denominations such as this and even to 0.05 BTC or 0.01 BTC (such as Microsoul), as 0.05 BTC in late 2013 was the dollar-equivalent of several BTC when Casascius first started to make coins.

The coin uses the same size hologram as the series 3 0.5 BTC coin, but lacks 'laser rimming' which the series 3 1 BTC coin features. These coins were sold in rolls of 20, meaning they ended up in relatively few hands.

The seven remaining unredeemed coins that were funded in 2012 are extremely rare, and are likely held by some of the first buyers.

Casascius Physical Bitcoin

Series 2 0.5 BTC 2013

Manufacturer: Casascius
Year: 2013
Denomination: 0.5 BTC
Type: PF

Load Year	Total	Unopened
2011		
2012		
2013	2,959	2,836
2014	125	125
Total	**3,084**	**2,961**

Material: Brass
Diameter: 25.4 mm
Thickness: 1.5 mm
Weight: 5.55 g
Country: USA
Best Grade: MS-68

On February 17, 2013, Casascius released these coins saying "This is being added due to the rise in bitcoin value". The price of Bitcoin had risen from under 14 USD to nearly 30 USD within a couple of weeks.

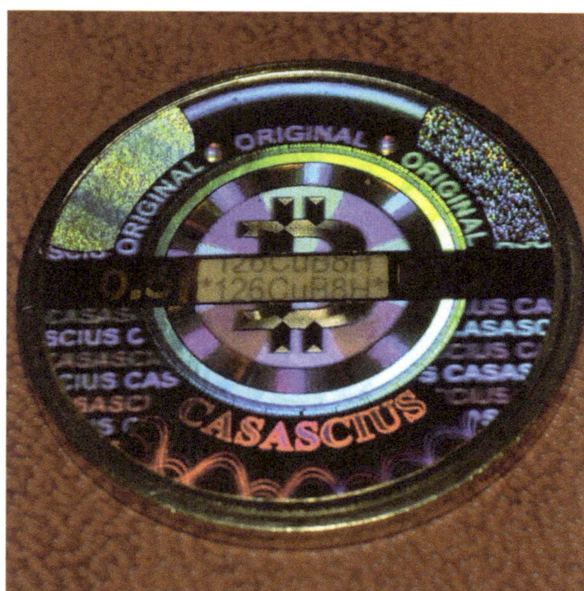

As with the 2013 series 2 1 BTC coins, there is 'lobe' on the private key and its pit to ensure correct positioning.

It is known that at least 42 0.5 BTC coins were late-funded in 2015 and 2016. It is unknown how many of them are of this variety.

Image Credits (clockwise): Howard Kesselman, Unknown

1. "THE FIRST OF THE 2013 1BTC COINS HAVE GONE OUT" Link: https://casascius.wordpress.com/2013/02/17/the-first-of-the-2013-1btc-coins-have-gone-out/

Casascius Physical Bitcoin

Series 2 0.5 BTC 2013 'Void Coin'

Manufacturer: Casascius
Year: 2013
Denomination: 0.5 BTC
Type: UF

Load Year	Total	Unopened
2011		
2012		
2013	N/A	N/A
2014		
Total	**N/A**	**N/A**

Material: Brass
Diameter: 25.4 mm
Thickness: 1.5 mm
Weight: 5.55 g
Country: USA
Best Grade: MS-66

These coins were given out to the press as gifts. They are different than typical 0.5 BTC Brass coins in that they have no public or private key, but instead display a repeating "VOID" in the window. These were shown in the movie *The Rise and Rise of Bitcoin* and were custom made in order not to compromise the private keys while these coins were being assembled on screen. While it is uncertain how many of these were created, it is estimated that roughly 12 were made and given to the press. It is unknown how many survive today as these may well have been discarded by unknowing recipients who were not collectors, especially considering that these coins contained no bitcoin. A search was conducted by Jon Allen (Bitcointalk.org user 'Eodguy149'), who got in touch with several members of the media who were associated with the film. He was able to locate three coins by this method.

The coin shown in the picture above is the actual coin owned by the producer, Ben Bledsoe, from the movie.

Image Credits (clockwise): Howard Kesselman, Jon Allen

Casascius Physical Bitcoin

Aluminum Promotional Coin

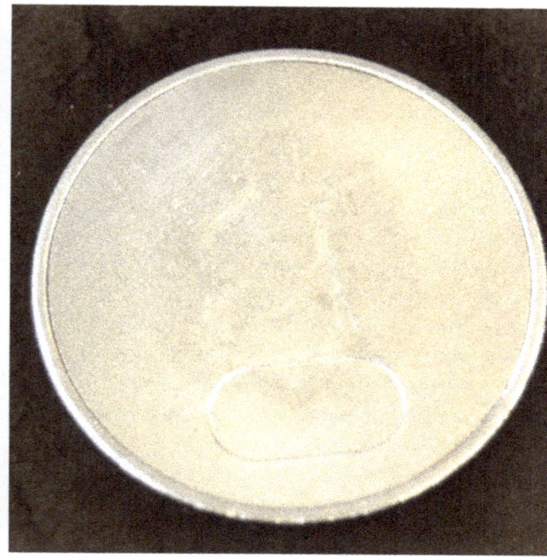

Manuf.: Casascius
Year: 2013
Denomination: BTC
Type: DIY

Version	Mintage
Plain	
Gold	
Red	
Purple	
Blue	
Green	
TOTAL	**80,000**

Material: Aluminum
Diameter: 32 mm
Thickness: 1.3 mm
Weight: 2.7 g
Country: USA

Image Credits (clockwise): Unknown (all)

These light and cheap coins are the only non-denominated Casascius coins, and come with no hologram stickers or private keys. There is a slight indent on the back to make storing a private key under a personal sticker easier.

One popular function of the coins is for use as personal business cards; simply create a sticker of your contact info and put it on the back. This has been utilized by some Bitcoin companies.

Perhaps unexpectedly, these coins have been used as a medium by other coin producers to create pre-funded or unfunded physical crypto-currency for commercial purposes. These include SerpCoin, Cryptofreeze, AussieBTC, and others.

They are sold in packages of 500, and are the only item available through Casascius after normal production and sale of coins ended.

These coins come in different colors, though the majority are plain aluminum.

Casascius Physical Bitcoin

Series 2 0.5 BTC 2013 'Silver Error'

Manufacturer: Casascius
Year: 2013
Denomination: 0.5 BTC
Type: PF

Load Year	Total	Unopened
2011		
2012		
2013	45*	45*
2014		
Total	**45**	**45***

Material: .999 Silver
Diameter: 30 mm
Thickness: 2.7 mm
Weight: 0.5 ozt
Country: USA
Best Grade: MS-68

"In addition we produced 45 half-BTC coins with the series-2 sticker which were not numbered into these rolls. These were available to those who made initial orders, though are no longer available for sale"

The coins were created to avoid wasting leftover series 2 holograms. They were sold in rolls of 12.

*It is assumed that none of these coins have been opened, as those receiving them likely understood their rarity and only two out of all silver 0.5 BTC coins are known to have been opened.

Image Credits (clockwise): unknown (all)

1. "STATUS ON SILVER COINS (JULY 23)" Link: https://casascius.wordpress.com/2013/07/23/status-on-silver-coins-july-23/

Casascius Physical Bitcoin

Series 3 0.5 BTC 2013

Manufacturer: Casascius
Year: 2013
Denomination: 0.5 BTC
Type: PF

Load Year	Total	Unopened
2011		
2012		
2013	871	869
2014	15	15
Total	**886**	**884**

Material: .999 Silver
Diameter: 30 mm
Thickness: 2.7 mm
Weight: 0.5 ozt
Country: USA
Best Grade: MS-70

Released alongside the series 3 1 BTC 2013 coin, these were sold in rolls of 12. Unlike their 1 BTC counter-parts, these (like the 0.1 BTC coin) series 3 holograms do not utilize 'laser rimming' as a security measure.

It is known that at least 42 additional 0.5 BTC coins are late-funded (LF) in 2015 and 2016. It is unknown how many of them are of this silver variety. It is unknown if any LF 'Silver Error' coins exist.

Image Credits (clockwise): Jon Allen, Unknown

Casascius Physical Bitcoins

Series 2 10 BTC 2012

Manufacturer: Casascius
Year: 2012
Denomination: 10 BTC
Type: PF

Load Year	Total	Unopened
2011	96*	78*
2012	290*	258*
2013	103*	99*
2014		
2015	4*	4*
Total	**493***	**439***

Material: .999 Silver
Diameter: 39 mm
Thickness: 3 mm
Weight: 1 ozt
Country: USA
Best Grade: MS-67

Image Credits (clockwise): Casascius (all)

Created in 2012, this was the first silver coin made by Casascius and a precursor to the 2013 series 3 line of silver coins. Four coins were funded in 2015.

This design builds upon the back of the Casascius 25 BTC coins, resulting in a smooth design that looks good in silver. Very similar designs are found in the coins of Lealana and Cryptolator. The 0's and 1's spell out 'Bitcoin: an idea too big to fail' in binary.

The same size and weight as the later 1 BTC silver coin, it is significant to note the missing 'laser rimming' which is present in the 1 BTC silver coins as well as the Lealana 1 BTC Silver Bitcoin line. This coin came shipped within a plastic capsule, protecting it (especially the later 'Gold B' design with its less than superior plating) from wear.

*Mintage figures represent both series 2 and series 2 'Gold B' versions; specific numbers are unknown, but the 'Gold B' is assumed to be more rare. It can be speculated that a total of 500 were minted.

Casascius Physical Bitcoin

Series 2 10 BTC 2012 'Gold B'

Manufacturer: Casascius
Year: 2012
Denomination: 10 BTC
Type: PF

Load Year	Total	Unopened
2011	96*	78*
2012	290*	258*
2013	103*	99*
2014		
2015	4*	4*
Total	**493***	**439***

Material: .999 Silver
Diameter: 39 mm
Thickness: 3 mm
Weight: 1 ozt
Country: USA
Best Grade: MS-67

Image Credits (clockwise): Casascius (all)

This coin is the same as the series 2 10 BTC 2012 version, albeit with a gold plating added over the Bitcoin sign. It is notable that this coin (this specific image) is proudly displayed by Casascius as his Bitcointalk.org thumbnail image, and is prominently visible on his website. It could be argued that this is among the most visually appealing of Mike Caldwell's work.

The Quality of the gold plating is said to be less than ideal, and was improved upon in the series 3 1 BTC 2013 'Gold Rim' coins. Since these coins were shipped inside capsules, the plating is not an issue as long as they remain inside.

*Mintage figures represent both series 2 and series 2 'Gold B' versions; specific numbers are unknown, but the 'Gold B' is assumed to be more rare. It can be speculated that a total of 500 were minted.

Casascius Physical Bitcoin

Series 1 25 BTC 2011 'Error'

Manufacturer: Casascius
Year: 2011
Denomination: 25 BTC
Type: PF

Load Year	Total	Unopened
2011	338	202
2012	5	4
2013	2	2
2014		
Total	**345**	**208**

Material: Gold plated alloy
Diameter: 44.5 mm
Thickness: 3 mm
Weight: ~1.2 oz
Country: USA
Best Grade: MS-67

Image Credits (clockwise): Charlie Lee (all)

Made in a different style than Casascius' other coins, this 25 BTC piece is iconic. It's black lacquered text stands out and is easy to read, and the raised B exudes confidence. It has been frequently displayed in the media in articles relating to Bitcoin, most notably during the extensive coverage of the November 2013 price surge.

On the reverse, the 0's and 1's spell out "You asked for change, we gave you coins" in binary, a reference to the 'change' Bitcoin might bring to the world economy and Caldwell's role in advancing it by his production of coins. Many coin producers have drawn inspiration and utilized a similar 'binary edge' design on their coins.

As far as public perception goes, this may be the most easily recognizable 'bitcoin' along with the series 2 1 BTC 2013 and series 3 1 BTC 2013 'Gold Rim'.

2012 and 2013 funded versions are extremely rare.

Casascius Physical Bitcoin

Series 2 25 BTC 2011

Manufacturer: Casascius
Year: 2011
Denomination: 25 BTC
Type: PF

Load Year	Total	Unopened
2011	29	19
2012	197	143
2013	260	194
2014	1	1
Total	**487**	**357**

Material: Gold plated alloy
Diameter: 44.5 mm
Thickness: 3 mm
Weight: ~1.2 oz
Country: USA
Best Grade: MS-67

The same coin as the series 1 25 BTC, this version features the series 2 hologram for added security.

Somewhat ironically, only a small fraction were actually funded in 2011 as the year on the coin implies, making those ones very scarce.

Image Credits (clockwise): Charlie Lee, Unknown

Casascius Physical Bitcoin

Series 1 1,000 BTC 2011 'Prototype' Gold Coin

Manuf.	Casascius
Year	2011
Denom.	1,000 BTC
Type	BF
Mintage	1
Material	.999 Gold
Diameter	30 mm
Thickness	2.8 mm (est.)
Weight	1 ozt
Country	USA

This is the rarest and most valuable Casascius coin. Being the first gold coin produced by Casascius, this was only meant to be a prototype and remain in Mr. Caldwell's ownership. He did however sell it to a buyer he met at a conference, who was unable to wait for a new coin to be minted considering that he was not based in the USA.

The pictured coin was sold by the original buyer for 1,000,000 USD in November 2013, the highest price ever paid for any bitcoin related item. If the value of 1 BTC were ever to approach 10,000 USD, this coin could potentially become the most valuable coin ever sold.

Image Credits (clockwise): JJC

Casascius Physical Bitcoin

Series 1 1,000 BTC 2011 Gold Coin

Manuf.	Casascius
Year	2011
Denom.	1,000 BTC
Type	BF
Mintage	~7*
Material	.999 Gold
Diameter	30 mm
Thickness	2.8 mm (est.)
Weight	1 ozt
Country	USA

*Estimated total of series 1 and series 2 gold coins

This coin was released in December 2011, when the total price of the coin, including the 1,000 BTC, was only about 5,000 USD. The Casascius 1,000 BTC coin was the first gold coin funded with crypto-currency.

The coin pictured is the only one known to be funded in 2011, discounting the prototype coin. It is not known if it is the only series 1 gold coin. The first-bits for this coin are laser-engraved on the upper part of the hologram, making it impossible for the address to be manipulated. As with the prototype, 'laser rimming' is not utilized for this coin.

Image Credits (clockwise): Casascius

Casascius Physical Bitcoin

Series 2 1,000 BTC 2011 Gold Coin

Manuf.	Casascius
Year	2011, 2012
Denom.	1,000 BTC
Type	BF
Mintage	~7*
Material	.999 Gold
Diameter	30 mm
Thickness	2.8 mm (est.)
Weight	1 ozt
Country	USA

*Estimated total of series 1 and series 2 gold coins

Made-to-order through a local mint, the Casascius gold coins were offered for about 200 USD above the gold spot price in addition to the buyer supplying the required 1,000 BTC, technically making them 'BF' instead of 'PF' coins.

The total number of coins produced and sold is known to be at least seven, of which two or more have been redeemed.

The series 2 coin features 'laser rimming' as an additional safeguard, and the hologram is engraved with '1000 BTC' to signal that it is funded.

Image Credits (clockwise): JJC

Casascius Physical Bitcoin

Series 1 100 BTC 2011 Bar

Manufacturer: Casascius
Year: 2011
Denomination: 100 BTC
Type: PF

Load Year	Total	Unopened
2011	56	16
2012	1	1
2013		
2014		
Total	**57**	**17**

Material: Gold plated alloy
Diameter: 80 x 40 mm
Thickness: 6 mm
Weight: 118 g (in wrap)
Country: USA

When the first bar was funded in November 2011, its contents would have been worth about 350 USD. For this reason it is quite understandable why two-thirds of owners rushed to redeem their bars in order to sell their precious contents as the value of BTC rose. As far as Casascius coins go, it is normal for the percentage of redeemed coins to be relatively low; the opposite is true when it comes to bars. Bars have a very high rate of redemption. This might be caused by a presumption that they were not as collectible or valuable as coins. The 'purchase price' (premium) of bars was a low percentage of the actual value contained in them, as opposed to coins (a 5 BTC coin was sold for 6 BTC; a 20 percent premium).

Image Credits: Steven Steiner

Casascius Physical Bitcoin

Series 2 100 BTC 2011 Bar

Manufacturer: Casascius
Year: 2011
Denomination: 100 BTC
Type: PF

Load Year	Total	Unopened
2011	29	11
2012	35	23
2013	22	21
2014		
Total	**86**	**55**

Material: Gold plated alloy
Diameter: 80 x 40 mm
Thickness: 6 mm
Weight: 118 g (in wrap)
Country: USA

Like its predecessor, the series 2 bar comes stamped with '100 BTC' below the hologram. This bar had the largest production of the denominated Casascius bars, with the most unopened specimens still remaining. The photo on the left demonstrates the back of a bar that is still in its original plastic wrap. All Casascius bars are identical on the back with a smooth brass surface.

Image Credits (clockwise): Bitcointalk.org user 'hyphymikey', Elias Ahonen

Casascius Physical Bitcoin

Series 2 100 BTC 2011 'Unfunded Bar'

Manuf.	Casascius
Year	2011
Denom.	100 BTC
Type	UF
Mintage	8
Material	Gold Pl. Alloy
Diameter	80 x 40 mm
Thickness	6 mm
Weight	118 g (in wrap)
Country	USA

These 'Non-2FA' 100 BTC bars are limited to a mintage of only eight pieces, none of which have been funded. To uniquely identify them as unfunded bars, these bars come with a 'ZERO BTC' etched hologram which is intentionally placed upside down. Additionally a small red dot was placed by the first-bits to further differentiate the hologram.

Image Credits: Took Groth

Casascius Physical Bitcoin

Series 2 100 BTC 2011 '2FA Unfunded Bar'

Manuf.	Casascius
Year	2011
Denom.	100 BTC
Type	UF
Mintage	4
Material	Gold Pl. Alloy
Diameter	80 x 40 mm
Thickness	6 mm
Weight	118 g (in wrap)
Country	USA

These bars were created from 100 BTC bars that were not funded or sold.

In order for Mr. Caldwell to confidently sell unfunded bars that were stamped with '100 BTC', he came up with the idea to add a laser-engraved 'ZERO BTC' directly onto the hologram to make it clear that the intact hologram was not interpreted to mean that the bars contained 100 BTC. Only four 2FA 100 BTC bars were made, none of which were funded at the time of purchase. In addition to the 'ZERO BTC' engraving, '2factor' is also engraved onto the upper half of the hologram.

These four bars are some of the rarest Casascius Bitcoin-denominated items with the exception of the unique Prototype 1,000 BTC Gold Coin, two 500 BTC Bars, and unique 1,000 BTC 2FA Unfunded Bar.

Image Credits: Bitcointalk.org user 'Bitguy101'

Casascius Physical Bitcoin

Series 1 500 BTC 2011 Bar

Manufacturer: Casascius
Year: 2011
Denomination: 500 BTC
Type: PF

Load Year	Total	Unopened
2011	1	1
2012	1	0
2013		
2014		
Total	**2**	**1**

Material: Gold plated alloy
Diameter: 80 x 40 mm
Thickness: 6 mm
Weight: 118 g (in wrap)
Country: USA

Considering that only one of these bars remain in an un-redeemed state, it will likely fetch the highest amount over face value compared to any other Casascius item if it is ever sold.

Unlike the normal series 1 first-bits that are printed on the hologram with an ink-jet printer, this bar has them added on with a laser to ensure that it cannot wear off or be erased. In addition, there are laser engraved '500 BTC' markings on the hologram in the same size and font as the same marking appears below the hologram on the bar itself.

Image Credits (clockwise): Steven Steiner (all)

Casascius Physical Bitcoin

Series 1 1000 BTC 2011 Bar

Manufacturer: Casascius
Year: 2011
Denomination: 1,000 BTC
Type: PF

Load Year	Total	Unopened
2011	12	2
2012	4	1
2013		
2014		
Total	**16**	**3**

Material: Gold plated alloy
Diameter: 80 x 40 mm
Thickness: 6 mm
Weight: 118 g (in wrap)
Country: USA

With less then 20 percent of the bars left un-redeemed, this bar is among the most elusive and valuable of the Casascius bars. '1000 BTC' and 'One Thousand Bitcoins' is laser printed on the bar (in the same manner as on the 500 BTC bar), instead of stamped like on the 100 BTC versions.

In February 2014, Casascius sold a redeemed bar on eBay for 3,850 USD, with all proceeds going to the Electronic Frontier Foundation.

The lower image is actually of an unfunded bar, but it demonstrates detail as there are few available photos of funded 1,000 BTC bars.

Image Credits (clockwise): Casascius, Bitcointalk.org user 'Bitguy101'

Casascius Physical Bitcoin

Series 2 1,000 BTC 2011 '2FA Unfunded Bar'

Manuf.	Casascius
Year	2011
Denom.	1,000 BTC
Type	UF
Mintage	1
Material	Gold Pl. Alloy
Diameter	80 x 40 mm
Thickness	6 mm
Weight	118 g (in wrap)
Country	USA

The 2FA 1,000 BTC bar is one of a kind. It has 'ZERO BTC' engraved on to the hologram. '2factor' is also engraved on to the hologram. It is a rarer counterpart to the series 2 100 BTC '2FA' bar

Image Credits: Bitcointalk.org user 'Bitguy101'

Casascius Physical Bitcoin

Series 2 2011 'Storage Bar'

Manuf.	Casascius
Year	2011
Denom.	BTC
Type	UF
Mintage	
Material	Gold Pl. Alloy
Diameter	80 x 40 mm
Thickness	6 mm
Weight	118 g (in wrap)
Country	USA

These bars were the first 'empty' item released by Casascius. They function like any physical Casascius coin in that Bitcoin can be sent to it using the first-bits, but redeemed only by removing the hologram.

Image Credits: Casascius

Casascius Physical Bitcoin

Series 2 2011 '2FA Storage Bar'

Manuf.	Casascius
Year	2011
Denom.	BTC
Type	UF
Mintage	
Material	Gold Pl. Alloy
Diameter	80 x 40 mm
Thickness	6 mm
Weight	118 g (in wrap)
Country	USA

The 2-Factor Storage Bar uses complex two factor authentication to access the stored BTC value once it is sent to the bar. These bars have their public address laser printed onto them, as well as 'casascius.com/2factor' which explains how the bars work.

In order to redeem the bar, one must not only tear the hologram to retrieve the private key, but combine it with another code provided at purchase. If a 2-Factor bar is sold, the seller will have the other part of the code, but is not able to access the funds as long as the hologram is intact.

For an unknown reason, all the first-bits appear to be intentionally obscured by black pen markings.

Image Credits (clockwise): Elias Ahonen (all)

Casascius Physical Bitcoin

10,000 LTC 2011 Bar

Acrylic LTC 2011

The most mysterious Casascius product is the 10,000 LTC bar, of which virtually nothing is known. The only available clue is this extremely poor quality photo, which does nothing more than confirm that Casascius once produced a bar with '10000 LTC | *One Thousand Litecoins*' written across it in the same format as for other high-denomination bars. It is not known how many were produced or if any were funded or sold.

The most 'odd' Casascius creation is the acrylic Litecoin round. They consist of acrylic 'rounds' laser-engraved with the Litecoin 'L' logo. It is not known how many exist, but the number is not likely to be above two dozen. Unlike all other coins and bars, these are made of transparent acrylic. The pictured rounds were given to CharlieLee along with a 100,000 LTC bar. Charlie Lee is an influential figure in the crypto-currency space, having been the creator of Litecoin.

10,000 LTC Bar

Manuf.	Casascius
Year	2011
Denom.	10,000 LTC
Type	
Mintage	
Material	Gold Pl. Alloy
Diameter	40 mm
Thickness	6 mm
Weight	118 g (in wrap)
Country	USA

Acrylic LTC round

Manuf.	Casascius
Year	2011
Denom.	LTC
Type	Round
Mintage	<50
Material	Acrylic
Diameter	
Thickness	
Weight	
Country	USA

Image Credits: Unknown, Charlie Lee

Casascius Physical Bitcoin

Series 1 100,000 LTC 2011 Bar

Manuf.	Casascius
Year	2011
Denom.	100,000 LTC
Type	PF
Mintage	1
Material	Gold Pl. Alloy
Diameter	80 x 40 mm
Thickness	6 mm
Weight	118 g (in wrap)
Country	USA

The Litecoin bar is one of a kind and was created specially for Charlie Lee, the creator of Litecoin. The loaded value '100,000 LTC' is laser-printed below the series 1 hologram. This is the only coin or bar that Casascius is known to have been funded with a non-bitcoin crypto-currency.

Below: close-up of an series 1 hologram

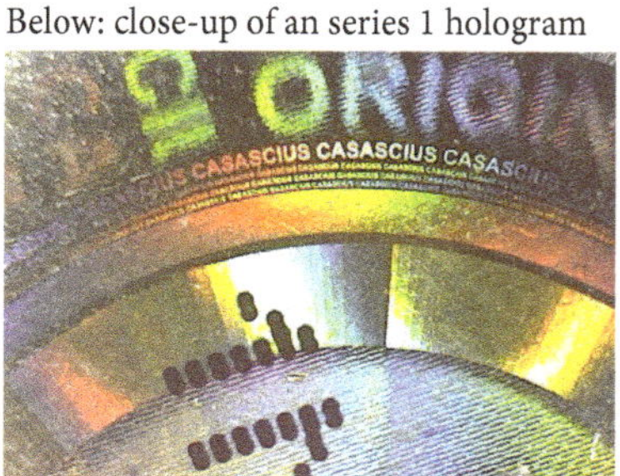

Image Credits: Charlie Lee, Bitcointalk.org user 'etotheipi'

Casascius Physical Bitcoin

St. Petersburg Bitcoin Bowl Coin

Manuf.	Casascius
Year	2014
Denom.	BTC
Type	Round
Mintage	2,000*
Material	.999 Silver
Diameter	39 mm
Thickness	3 mm
Weight	1 ozt
Country	USA

* 2,000 were minted. Only 850 were put into circulation, and the remainder were melted down.

To much surprise, this coin was announced on December 23rd, 2014 as a commemorative coin for the St. Petersburg Bitcoin Bowl, a Florida college football championship sponsored by BitPay which is a leading Bitcoin payment processor. One of the coins was used for the coin toss at the game's kickoff.

"Adorned with gold plating on the polished rim, the Bitcoin B, and the bowl logo, this is the only coin to be released by Casascius in the 2014 calendar year"[1].

They were offered for sale online at $100 each.

Image Credits (clockwise): Bitcointalk.org user 'bitcoininformation', Took Groth

1. '2014 Casascius St. Petersburg Bowl Bitcoin Coin' Link: https://bitcointalk.org/index.php?topic=903503.0

Chinese Businessman

Gold Coin

Manuf.	Chinese Businessman
Year	2014
Denom.	1 BTC
Type	PF
Mintage	101
Material	.999 Gold
Diameter	
Thickness	
Weight	1 oz
Country	China

Photos and information of this round were first posted on a Chinese Bitcoin news portal by an individual claiming to have been commissioned to produce the coins. Not much is known about these coins, but because there are said to be up to 101 solid gold specimens, their existence is noteworthy. They were minted by a Chinese businessman (hence the producer name; no official name is available), and destined for a private collection as opposed to public sale. It is believed the QR code on the back is the private key, unique to each coin. It has been claimed that the coins are somehow backed by physical gold, which is supported by the text on the back. Something very interesting about the coins is that the serial number appears to not be engraved and instead seems to be part of the original strike. If this is the case, these coins would be incredibly expensive to individually produce.

The front of the coin features a rather oddly laid out world map, with a solid 'B' in the center. The statement 'Open Source P2P Money' is prominent at the bottom. The back states "The World's First Gold-Backed Physical Bitcoins' and features imagery relating to mining and encryption on a circuit-board pattern similar to the style used by MJB Monetary Metals. The stated denomination of 1 BTC is also obvious.

Image Credits (clockwise): Chinese Businessman (all)

CoinBull

Gold Plated Coin

Manuf.	CoinBull
Year	2015
Denom.	BTC
Type	PF
Mintage	
Material	Gold Pl. Alloy
Diameter	50 mm
Thickness	4 mm
Weight	53 g
Country	USA

CoinBull is an online store selling precious metal bullion as well as BTC and LTC. Both for promotional purposes and to serve as an effective medium to store BTC, the 'Coinbull Crypto Coin' was released as a way to allow 'physical delivery' of BTC and LTC.

The face of the coin is dominated by the head of a bull, which is naturally inspired by the name of the company. The name itself is a combination of two concepts: precious metal 'bullion' and a 'bullish' view on both precious metals and crypto-currency. Though the name does suggest it, the coin does not contain precious metals beyond the silver and gold plating. The Latin phrase 'In Utroque Partus' means 'Prepared for Anything', perhaps suggesting financial preparedness for the eventual collapse of government-issued money. This interpretation is likely to be correct, considering that the company's slogan is "bullish on coins, bearish on currency". The back sticker has no hologram, but does include a printed public key and corresponding QR code, with a private key behind it.

Image Credits (clockwise): Howard Kesselman, CoinBull

CoinedBits

Bitcoin 2010 Limited Edition Solid Copper

Manuf.	CoinedBits
Year	2015
Denom.	BTC
Type	Round
Mintage	
Material	Copper
Diameter	39 mm
Thickness	3 mm
Weight	1 oz
Country	USA

This round is stamped with the year 2010, but it was released in 2015. It is an antique copper version of the '2009' (also released in 2015) CoinedBits round. It uses the same front design as the other CoinedBits rounds, but the back has a unique image referring to Bitcoin mining. The rocks that the miner is chipping away at are embedded with binary code, signifying the fact that it is not rock but data that 'mining' is concerned with. Small 'bitcoins' are seen emerging from the 'data rock' as a result of the miner's efforts. The CoinedBits website address is displayed.

Image Credits (clockwise): CoinedBits (all)

CoinedBits

Physical Bitcoin

Manuf.	CoinedBits
Year	2011
Denom.	BTC
Type	Round
Mintage	
Material	Gold Pl. Brass
Diameter	39 mm
Thickness	3 mm
Weight	1 oz
Country	USA

This is the first CoinedBits round, released in 2011. Its front design is very much classic, and has influenced later coins. A notable example is the Finite By Design 'Real Bitcoin' coin, which is nearly identical. The back has a smaller 'B' along with the CoinedBits website. A blank bar exists at the bottom.

Bitcoin 2009 Limited Edition 18K Gold Plated

Manuf.	CoinedBits
Year	2015
Denom.	BTC
Type	Round
Mintage	
Material	Gold Pl. Brass
Diameter	39 mm
Thickness	3 mm
Weight	1 oz
Country	USA

While '2009' (the year Bitcoin was launched) is stamped on the front, the round was released in 2015, and was likely minted that year. The round differs from the 2011 round by not having a 'blank bar' on the back, with the year '2009' appearing in its place.

Image Credits (clockwise): CoinedBits (all)

Coinographic

Coinographic was founded in early 2014 by Mark Hamilton in the UK, with the goal to bring high quality physical Litecoins to the market. The coins produced were of a very high quality, with high quality custom wooden display boxes being a particularly stand-out offering. The company hosted several design competitions, with the winning designs being decided by voting and subsequently put into production. As a result of this community input, the coins developed can be seen as being accurate reflections of those interested in physical crypto-currency. One such competition to design a 2oz .999 gold 5 BTC coin (with the prize being the #001/100 funded coin worth several thousand dollars in ‘raw material’) became quite heated with accusations of rigged voting and plagiarism between the leading contestants. At over $240,000 for the raw gold and an additional ~$200,000 for the BTC required to fund the coins, this was projected to be the most ambitious project in physical crypto-currency at the time. Though the production of the coin was announced to have begun in October 2014, it was never released (along with several other coins for which pre-orders existed) and the contest winner did not receive any prize. Coinographic did post a photo of a copper prototype created by the mint, which is pictured on the right.

In January 2015 after prolonged speculation, Mr. Hamilton announced “An unfortunate chain of events has led us to a situation where we can no longer operate as a business. Low volume sales, coupled with a large decline in the value of digital currency have left the business crippled”.[1] This announcement was only the beginning of many issues, as it became apparent that the company was unable to honor over $40,000 in pre-orders or issue monetary refunds because the money was spent on molds, dies, prototypes, holograms, and boxes. Though Mark offered to use unsold inventory to provide a partial refund to per-ordering customers, it was later revealed that the amount of inventory was very low and not nearly sufficient, inspiring further accusations of misrepresentation.

Image Credits: Coinographic (all)

1. " Calling you forth, Coinographic" *Bitcoin Talk* 29 January 2015. Link: https://bitcointalk.org/index.php?topic=938192.15

A further issue came to light when it was alleged that some 'funded' 25 LTC coins that were shipped months earlier were not actually funded (they were meant to receive funding once the customer received them) like they were supposed to. Noah Luis (creator of Lealana) publicly suggested that all Coinographic coins may be compromised (because there was allegedly no reason to believe that Mark had not retained the private keys and ability to take back the LTC inside coins) and encouraged everyone to redeem their Coinographic coins. Noah was one of many prominent members of the collector community who were highly critical of the company's operations and apparent ethics..[1]

About three weeks after the initial announcement, Mark made a rather desperate statement in response to progressive calls for refunds. He said that "I personally have no money... I am struggling to put food on the table for my children. You can DOX me (my information freely available on the net), sue me or visit my house".[1]

On March 24th 2015, somebody moved the LTC balance of a sealed 25 LTC coin into a crypto-currency exchange. The coin was owned by Litecointalk.org user 'evilb', who several weeks later posted a dated picture of the obviously un-tampered coin with visible first-bits to confirm that the private key had not been removed. The only way this could have been accomplished is if the individual who assembled or otherwise handled the private keys kept copies of them for themselves. This is the first time that a physical crypto-coin has been compromised in this way, and demonstrates the inherent issue with the physical crypto-currency model.

Though Coinographic was initially well received by collectors, it failed in extraordinary fashion. As of writing, over $40,000 combined is owed to customers, with both civil legal actions and criminal charges pending against Mr. Hamilton.

While no proof exists, it is possible that the 2oz .999 Gold coins were minted, but not released from the mint likely due to lack of payment on part of Coinographic. If this is true, it means that one or more of the coins may surface one day. Even if they were produced, it is however likely that they would have all been melted down after a certain time-frame.

Image Credits: Coinographic

1. " COINOGRAPHIC IS A SCAMMER [CON-O-GRAPHIC]" Link: https://bitcointa.lk/threads/coinographic-is-a-scammer-con-o-graphic.422479/

Coinographic

1 LTC 2014 Production Coin

Manuf.	Coinographic
Year	2014
Denom.	1 LTC
Type	PF
Mintage	500
Material	Silver Plated
Diameter	37 mm
Thickness	3 mm
Weight	25 g
Country	UK

This coin borrows from the physical Litecoin design first minted by Lealana, as evidenced by the central section of the front (compare the photo of a Lealana coin on the right). The inner section appears inspired by a mechanical lock, which is used in a visual metaphor for the absolute security that a private key has. This implies that the coin is a secure medium of storage for Litecoins. Coin #001 was gifted to Charles Lee, the founder of Litecoin who gave high praise to the design. In line with the theme, the hologram features two keys crossed over the private key.

Image Credits (clockwise): Howard Kesselman (2)

Coinographic

10 LTC (Chikun Edition)

Manuf.	Coinographic
Year	2014
Denom.	10 LTC
Type	PF
Mintage	500
Material	.999 Silver
Diameter	38 mm
Thickness	3 mm
Weight	1 oz
Country	UK

The theme of this coin is 'Arise Chikun Arise'; the story of which is similar to the way users rallied around the 'Doge' meme. Someone in a Litecoin related chat linked a humorous YouTube video called 'Arise Chicken' as a metaphor for community member's patient waiting for the 'eventual' rise in LTC value. The 'meme' was so popular that the 'Chikun' (with a rocket strapped to its back) became an unofficial mascot for the currency, and the saying 'Arise Chicken Arise' began to be used as a sort of an Internet-age 'rain-dance' to encourage LTC value to increase.

Image Credits (clockwise): Howard Kesselman (all)

Coinographic

10 LTC (Litecoin Association Edition)

Manuf.	Coinographic
Year	2014
Denom.	10 LTC
Type	PF
Mintage	500
Material	.999 Silver
Diameter	38 mm
Thickness	3 mm
Weight	1 oz
Country	UK

A quick glance of this coin reminds one of a Ravenbit 'Node' coin, which employ a similar design (Compare to the small image of a 'Node' coin on the right). The idea that the design is trying to convey is that Litecoin's (like most other crypto-currencies') foundation is its large network which is de-centralized and distributed worldwide. The coin contains the text 'A Brighter Financial Future'. A very interesting thing to note is that the coin has standard UK silver markings, which convey official information about purity and year of production.

Image Credits (clockwise): Howard Kesselman (all)

Coinographic

25 LTC Limited Edition Coin

Manuf.	Coinographic
Year	2014
Denom.	25 LTC
Type	PF
Mintage	500*
Material	.999 Silver
Diameter	50 mm
Thickness	3 mm
Weight	2 oz
Country	UK

*It is estimated that only 100 coins were minted and 50 of those were funded.

The bull on this coin conveys a bullish (positive) outlook for Litecoin. The backside (and the nosering of the bull) features segments of chain, which represents the blockchain upon which Litecoin is based. The hologram is of a different design, with a circuit board outer pattern referring to technology and an inner Greco-Roman style pillared structure to indicate security. This coin is the first ever to fall victim to an alleged theft of contained value by the creator, to which all current Pre-Funded coins are ultimately vulnerable. After the 'situation', many of these coins were redeemed.

Image Credits (clockwise): Howard Kesselman (all)

Coldco.in

Physical Bitcoin Cold Storage Spy Coin

Manuf.	Coldco.in
Year	2014
Denom.	1 BTC
Type	UF
Mintage	100
Material	Gold Pl. Alloy
Diameter	39 mm
Thickness	3 mm
Weight	20 g
Country	USA

Image Credits (clockwise): Howard Kesselman (2), Coldco.in

The 'Physical Bitcoin Cold Storage Spy Coin' is unlike any other physical crypto-coin. It is designed to hide a private key, but it has no sticker or hologram nor engraved key. Instead, it actually opens up in a way that a piece of paper or even SD memory card can be put inside the coin thus hidden in plain sight! The 'spy coin' comes from the historical fact that similar hollow coins were used during the Cold War to hide secret messages or even conceal drugs which an agent could use to end their life upon capture. The name 'Cold Coin' refers to 'cold storage', which is the state of crypto-currency being stored in such a way that they are 'offline' and impervious to hacks or accidental computer damage. The front face of the coin consists of a Bitcoin 'B' which is covered in gears, whereas the backside displays several gears that remind one of a mechanical watch. All 100 coins are serialized.

The coin's categorization as 'unfunded' is valid since the design is intended to 'secure' a private key, though the lack of any security sticker means that the integrity of the stored private key (i.e., the fact that it has not been opened since being sealed) cannot be guaranteed.

Copperhead Bullion

Titanium Round

Manuf.	Copperhead Bullion
Year	
Denom.	BTC
Type	Round
Mintage	
Material	Titanium
Diameter	
Thickness	
Weight	1 oz
Country	USA

These Bitcoin themed titanium rounds are one of a set of eight, which are the first ever one ounce titanium rounds offered for sale. Other designs in the series are not related to Bitcoin, and are composed of images such as the Titanium element symbol and themes common in US currency like the American Buffalo, 'Walking Liberty', and 'Morgan Dollar'. What makes this set rather striking is that it so casually includes Bitcoin as one of several themes, with the issuing company having no Bitcoin affiliation. It can thus be interpreted as a sign that Bitcoin is being recognized by the mainstream, or at least by Copperhead's customer base, as a "ground-breaking digital currency that's taking the financial world by storm"[1] as it is described in the product description.

Image Credits (clockwise): Copperhead Bullion (all)

1. "Bitcoin 1 oz Titanium Round" Link: http://www.copperheadbullion.com/products/bitcoin-1-oz-titanium-round

Criptoe

Guldencoin

Manuf.	Criptoe
Year	2014
Denom.	5,000 NLG
Type	DIY
Mintage	250
Material	Gold Pl. Alloy
Diameter	44 mm
Thickness	3 mm
Weight	38 g
Country	Netherlands

These coins were produced in conjunction by several members of the Guldencoin development team. Guldencoin is an alternative crypto-currency, which was proclaimed to be the 'official crypto-currency of the Netherlands' by its creators. The name 'Guldencoin' is derived from the 'Dutch Guilder', which was the national currency unit before the introduction of the euro.

The front of the coin is designed to mimic the Dutch 1 Guilder coin (shown on the bottom left). The Guldencoin 'G' is presented on the front. The launch date of 'April 4th 2014' is displayed prominently, along with the denomination and serial number. The rim of the coin has a diamond cut pattern, giving it a 'golden' glimmer. The coins were sold for around 15 EUR each, with the lowest 50 serial numbers going for higher prices. The edge of the coin is engraved with the phrase "Betalen Met Guldencoin", which translates from Dutch to "Pay With Guldencoin".

Image Credits (clockwise): Took Groth, Howard Kesselman, Public Domain

Crypto Imperator

Crypto Imperator launched in June 2014, with a small batch of coins shipping from Spain. Their first coins were not denominated in Bitcoin, but Dogecoin which is an alternate digital currency with similar functions of Bitcoin.

Based on a meme, the DOGE currency itself was actually started as a joke in December 2013. It quickly gained widespread popularity and user-base reaching a market cap above 77 million USD in less than three months. From a market perspective, DOGE users were generally seen as being less serious and possessing smaller amounts of crypto-currency. Dogecoin was an effective catalyst in educating a larger amount of people about crypto-currency, providing an easy and fun entry-point.

From a market perspective, DOGE users were less likely to pay for luxurious coins made of precious metals. Instead, Crypto Imperator designed cheap coins that, at only $10, could be bought without much thought to serve as a keepsake or conversation pieces. When paying for a Crypto Imperator coin, payment and 'funding amount' were sent separately, but each coin was not directly funded by the buyer. For example, when purchasing three 10,000 doge coins, the customer would be asked to provide payment and shipping in one payment, and send 30,000 doge to a separate address.

Crypto Imperator has been successful in expanding their business. In addition to a BTC denominated coin and a 1oz silver 100,000 DOGE coin, Crypto Imperator has released a very small run of ten .999 Gold 1,000,000 DOGE coins, making them one of the very few manufacturers to mint solid gold crypto coins.

Image Credits (clockwise): Crypto Imperator (all)

Crypto Imperator

10,000 Doge Limited Ed.

Manuf.: Crypto Imperator
Year: 2014
Denomination: 10,000 DOGE
Type: PF, DIY

Version	Mintage
Serial (PF)	100
Non Serial (PF, DIY)	400
TOTAL	**500**

Material: Zinc Alloy
Diameter: 39 mm
Thickness: 2.5 mm
Weight: 25 g
Country: Spain

Crypto Imperator released it`s first coin in June 2014, aiming to provide a cheaper alternative in the market. Starting as low as $10 + 10,000 doge, it was easily the most affordable pre-funded coin at the time of release.

Following the tradition of 'Silver Wallets', the first 100 coins were numbered and sold on a first-come, first-serve basis for a $6 premium.

The hologram of this coin is notable, as it contains several layers of imagery, consisting of a rocket circling a moon with "TO THE MOON" text, "Crypto Imperator Original", and more. It was perhaps the most complicated hologram of all coins produced at the time of release.

Image Credits (clockwise): Elias Ahonen (2), Howard Kesselman (1)

Crypto Imperator

10,000 bits Bitcoin Ed.

Manuf.: Crypto Imperator
Year: 2014
Denomination: 0.01 BTC
Type: PF, DIY

Version	Mintage
Serial (PF)	100
Non Serial (PF, DIY)	400
TOTAL	**500**

Material: Zinc Alloy
Diameter: 39 mm
Thickness: 2.5 mm
Weight: 25 g
Country: Spain

This coin was introduced as a response to the success of the 10,000 DOGE coin. While the name 'Crypto Imperator', makes no reference to any specific crypto-currency, the Crypto Imperator hologram unquestionably has a 'Dogecoin' theme due to pop-culture references of 'To The Moon' written on it. The coin uses the same backside and hologram as the first release coin.

Notably, this is the first '0.01 BTC' coin represented as being '10,000 bits' (which is still accurate). The denomination ties this coin back to the initial Doge Coin due to both bearing the number '10,000'.

Image Credits (clockwise): Howard Kesselman (2), Crypto Imperator (1)

Crypto Imperator

100,000 Doge Silver Ed. 'SuperDoge'

Manuf.	Crypto Imper.
Year	2014
Denom.	100,000 DOGE
Type	PF
Mintage	25
Material	.999 Silver
Diameter	39 mm
Thickness	3 mm
Weight	1 ozt
Country	Spain

This coin was offered by email exclusively to the buyers of the 10,000 DOGE coin. Discounting material, it is identical to the 10,000 DOGE coin save for the denomination which is displayed on the bottom of the face. Like the two other coins, it uses the same mold and hologram for the back portion.

Image Credits (clockwise): Howard Kesselman (all)

Crypto Imperator

1/2 Troy Oz .999 Fine Gold 1 Million Dogecoin

Manuf.	Crypto Imper.
Year	2015
Denom.	1,000,000 DOGE
Type	PF
Mintage	10
Material	.999 Gold
Diameter	29.8 mm
Thickness	1.3 mm
Weight	0.5 ozt
Country	Spain

This coin was minted after getting enough pre-orders to cover the cost of production. It is the first ever case of a solid gold coin being minted for an 'alt-coin' (a crypto-currency other than Bitcoin).

While it bears a clear resemblance to the original Crypto Imperator DOGE coins, it has been modified so that the dog appears rich in a comical and stereotypical fashion. The coin as a whole is an excellent reflection of the culture around Dogecoin, which often makes light-hearted and humorous claims about dogecoins being worth more than gold and users becoming 'rich doges' one day as a result of their DOGE. This coin could indeed be seen as an extrapolation of the Dogecoin user-base to represent a 'doge' who has made 'such money' and become rich.

Image Credits (clockwise): Crypto Imperator (2), Bcointalk.org user 'gravitate'

Crypto Coin Warehouse

Paycoin Gold

Manuf.	Crypto Coin Warehouse
Year	2015
Denom.	XPY
Type	DIY
Mintage	
Material	Gold Pl. Brass
Diameter	39 mm
Thickness	3 mm
Weight	28 g
Country	USA

Crypto Coin Warehouse has made two DIY coins with a 'Paycoin' theme. Paycoin is an alternative crypto-currency, and these are the only coins to be made with a Paycoin theme. Since they are DIY, they can be funded with any currency that the owner chooses. The center of the coin features the Paycoin 'P' logo, and 'the people's money' which is the currency's motto. The backside has the coins currency code (XPY) at the bottom.

Paycoin Silver

Manuf.	Crypto Coin Warehouse
Year	2015
Denom.	XPY
Type	DIY
Mintage	
Material	Silver Pl. Brass
Diameter	39 mm
Thickness	3 mm
Weight	27 g
Country	USA

Paycoin launched in December 2014, and it soon reached a massive market cap of over 160 million USD. The currency is generally not seen as being successful, considering that the market cap is around $500,000 at the time of writing. The value of individual Paycoins has fallen from a high of 0.041 BTC to 0.00007408 BTC.

Image Credits (clockwise): Howard Kesselman (4), Crypto Coin Warehouse

Cryptofreeze

v1 Series 1

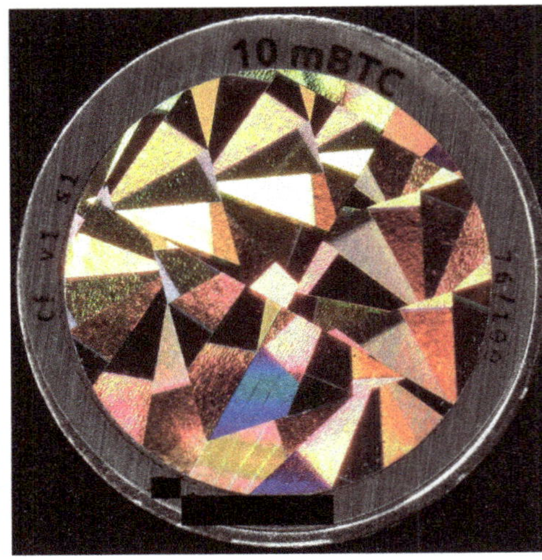

Manuf.	Cryptofreeze
Year	2014
Denom.	0.01 BTC
Type	UF
Mintage	100
Material	Aluminum
Diameter	31.8 mm
Thickness	1.6 mm
Weight	2.8 g
Country	USA

Cryptofreeze coins were inspired by the original 'Serpcoin' pre-funded coins. These coins are identical to Serpcoin's creations, except for the printed name and markings on the outer edge of the backside. An additional factor to take into account is that while these coins are denominated as 0.01 BTC, they are not pre-funded. It is interesting to observe that both types of coins actually use the exact same scratch-off hologram stickers. Counterfeiting is possibly a concern for these coins (as well as the similar coins made by Serpcoin), as all anyone would need to acquire the same stickers, an aluminum Casascius coin, and use a printer to create the markings on the side. Though the value of either coin is not yet at a level where such an act would be worthwhile, it is sensible to stay vigilant.

The 'Cryptofreeze' name clearly alludes to the idea that BTC loaded onto the coin will be in a secure 'frozen' state out of the reach of hackers.

Image Credits (clockwise): Howard Kesselman (all)

Cryptogifts

Peercoin Round

These Peercoin themed rounds were the first coins released by Cryptogifts, with sales being focused on the Peercointalk.org forum centered on the alternative crypto-currency. They are available with gold and silver plating (silver pictured below). The front has the 'P' logo with a green enamel leaf in the center, which symbolizes the environmentally friendly aspects of Peercoin (the mining process uses less electricity than Bitcoin). The words 'Peercoin | Digital Currency' are on the front rim, along with 'PPC', the abbreviation for the currency. The back has a similar theme, with 'Limited Edition | In Crypto We Trust', along with 'POS' which refers to Proof Of Stake (the algorithm of Peercoin). All 100 rounds are serialized.

Manufacturer: Cryptogifts
Year: 2014
Denomination: PPC
Type: Round

Material	Mintage
Gold Pl. Copper	100
Silver Pl. Copper	100
Total	**200**

Diameter: 30 mm
Thickness: 2 mm
Weight: 14 g
Country: USA

Image Credits (clockwise): Elias Ahonen (all)

Cryptogifts

I/O Round

Manufacturer: Cryptogifts
Year: 2014
Denomination: I/O
Type: Round

Material	Mintage
Gold Pl. Copper	100
Silver Pl. Copper	100
Total	**200**

Diameter: 30 mm
Thickness: 3 mm
Weight: 15 g
Country: USA

The I/O coins were the second of Cryptogifts' releases. Like the Peercoins, they are available in gold and silver plate with 100 serialized units of each. They are based on the alternative crypto-currency I/O Coin. They follow the same format as the Peercoin rounds, with an increased usage of enamel. Cryptogifts explained the choice to use enamel as opposed to paint, reasoning that enamel hardens very well and cannot be scratched off as opposed to paint which is known to chip easily. The front features the text 'WWW.IOCOIN.IO|Digital Currency', and the back is the same as for the Peercoin rounds except that 'I/O Coin' is specified.

Image Credits (clockwise): Elias Ahonen (all)

Cryptogifts

Gold BTC Round

Manuf.	Cryptogifts
Year	2014
Denom.	BTC
Type	Round
Mintage	100
Material	Gold Pl. Copper
Diameter	40 mm
Thickness	3 mm
Weight	28.6 g
Country	USA

The gold plated Bitcoin round is the largest Cryptogift round with a width of 40 mm. It has the prominent text 'Libertas | Equitas | Veritas | Bitcoin' (the Latin words mean Freedom, Equality, and Truth) suggesting that the words describe the values behind Bitcoin. These four words surround the central 'B' in a simple and classic design.

Silver LTC Round

Manuf.	Cryptogifts
Year	2015
Denom.	LTC
Type	Round
Mintage	100
Material	Gold Pl. Copper
Diameter	35 mm
Thickness	3 mm
Weight	21.1 g
Country	USA

This Litecoin is the most recent coin produced by Cryptogifts. Appropriately, it is plated in silver in reference to the theme of Litecoin (the Bitcoin round is plated gold in the same vein). The front has the text 'Vires In Numeris | Litecoins' and the Litecoin theme is virtually identical to similar coins created by Coinographic, Finite By Design, and Lealana. A somewhat differentiating factor is that it says 'Litecoins' instead of 'Litecoin', perhaps in error. The back is standard format, comparable to other Crytptogifts rounds with 'Litecoin', '2015', and the serial number out of 100.

Image Credits (clockwise): Elias Ahonen (all)

Cryptolator

In April 2014, Cryptolator announced the release of the "Cryptolator Unchained" coins. The first coin made available was limited to 140 coins and made of pure silver. Later, copper, Merlin Gold, 'antique copper', and 'antique brass' versions were released bearing the same 'Unchained' design. Cryptolator is based in Quebec, Canada and is run by Jonathan Leonard. Upon release of the brand it was initially stated that a new design would come out yearly, but as of printing, only the first design has been released.

The Cryptolator design is highly symbolic. It features a group of people empowered by Bitcoin using chains to pull down the supporting pillars of a burning central bank, as a pig and a dog with bags of 'fiat' money sit weeping at its ruined steps. On the capstone of the bank is an 'Illuminati eye' which is closed and crying. The chains which are used to pull down the supports of the current financial institution symbolize the 'blockchain' upon which Bitcoin is based. This symbolism reflects sentiments that permeate the bitcoin community; a belief that the present system of 'fiat' money controlled by central banks is flawed and inferior to the free-market logic upon which Bitcoin is built. The assumption of many in the Bitcoin community is that the monetary system will eventually collapse as it is made obsolete by a superior system. This broad discourse and conviction (and even hope) is displayed on Cryptolator coins in one thought-provoking image. As it goes, a picture says a thousand words. The weeping bankers who are presented as pigs and dogs were inspired by the 1977 Pink Floyd music album 'Animals' which uses animals to symbolize and critique the state of capitalistic society. This album was actually inspired by 'Animal Farm' by George Orwell.

The back side of the coin features the 'binary pattern' made popular by both Casascius and Lealana. Cryptolator's coins could be seen as adding something more to the market by replacing the 'simple' designs on some Casascius and Lealana coins with something much more appealing as a piece of art.

Cryptolator coins could be ordered in three configurations; multi-signature, single-key signature, or 'DIY.' Multi-signature and single-key coins come with an 'Original' marked hologram sealed by Cryptolator, while the holograms on 'DIY' coins are marked 'Personal' and are provided to the buyer as stickers. Most coins were not pre-funded prior to shipment, so the majority of Cryptolator coins do not contain any BTC value.

Image Credits (clockwise): Cryptolator

Cryptolator

Unchained Silver Series

Manufacturer: Cryptolator
Year: 2014
Denomination: 1 BTC
Type: PF, BF, DIY

Version	Mintage
Serial	120
Non Serial	20
TOTAL	**140**

Material: .999 Silver
Diameter: 39 mm
Thickness: 3 mm
Weight: 1 ozt
Country: Canada

This coin was the first to be released by Cryptolator. With a mintage of 140, 120 are numbered from 001 to 120 with the remaining 20 without serial numbers. Of these 20, four received unique engravings of 'Red', 'Green', 'Blue', and 'Yellow' and were auctioned on eBay to drum up interest in the coins and brand. The remaining 16 were each given unique 'non-serial identifiers' which were sold separately several months after the initial 120 sold out. A full list of 'non-serial identifiers' for Cryptolator coins is found in this section. The 'binary rim' design is inspired by visually similar coins by Casascius and Lealana, both pictured below.

Image Credits (clockwise): Elias Ahonen (2)

Cryptolator

Unchained Antique Bronze Series

Manuf.	Cryptolator
Year	2014
Denom.	0.1 BTC
Type	PF, UF
Mintage	25
Material	Ant. Bronze
Diameter	39 mm
Thickness	3 mm
Weight	27 g
Country	Canada

The 'Unchained' coins were made with four other metallic compositions in addition to silver. The most common of these is copper, of which 480 are serialized and 20 have 'non-serial identifiers'. Similarly, 20 of the 120 'Merlin Gold' coins are un-serialized. The Merlin Gold coins were never sold directly by Cryptolator, but rather exclusively via another member of the Bitcointalk.org forum who acted as a US distributor who had some of the lower numbers graded prior to sale. The Antique Copper coin pictured on the next page is the only specimen in which the hologram is significantly crooked.

Image Credits (clockwise): Elias Ahonen (all)

Cryptolator

Unchained Merlin Gold Series

Manuf.	Cryptolator
Year	2014
Denom.	0.1 BTC
Type	PF, UF
Mintage	120
Material	Merlin Gold
Diameter	39 mm
Thickness	3 mm
Weight	27 g
Country	Canada

Unchained Antique Copper Series

Manuf.	Cryptolator
Year	2014
Denom.	0.1 BTC
Type	PF, UF
Mintage	25
Material	Ant. Copper
Diameter	39 mm
Thickness	3 mm
Weight	27 g
Country	Canada

Unchained Copper series

Manuf.	Cryptolator
Year	2014
Denom.	0.1 BTC
Type	PF, UF, DIY
Mintage	520
Material	Copper
Diameter	39 mm
Thickness	3 mm
Weight	27 g
Country	Canada

Image Credits (clockwise): Howard Kesselman (1), Elias Ahonen (5)

Non-serialized Cryptolator coins

The non-serial 'identifiers' engraved on to 60 of the 790 Cryptolator can be seen as an additional opportunity for artistic expression. These are classed into six series of 'USA', 'Colors', 'Elements', 'Animals', 'Sins', and 'Other'. The 'USA' series celebrates the US distributor of the Merlin coins, while the 'Animals' ties to the reference of the pig and dog on the coin as explained earlier.

USA	Colors	Elements	Animals	Sins	Other
USA1	Red	Fire	Dogs	Lust**	000
USA2	Green	Water	Pigs	Greed**	Liberté*
USA3	Blue	Wind	Sheep	Pride**	Hope*
USA4	Yellow	Earth			1981***
USA5					

* ONLY on 1 BTC Silver Coin.
** NOT on 1 BTC Silver Coin.
*** Kept personally by Jonathan Leonard (* also applies).

Clockwise:
'Fire' on a Merlin Gold coin.
'Roll #2' of 25 Copper coins sold along with Antique Copper, Antique Bronze, and Merlin Gold coins at auction.
The complete 'Unchained' collection..
An Antique Bronze coin without a hologram attached, showing the pit.

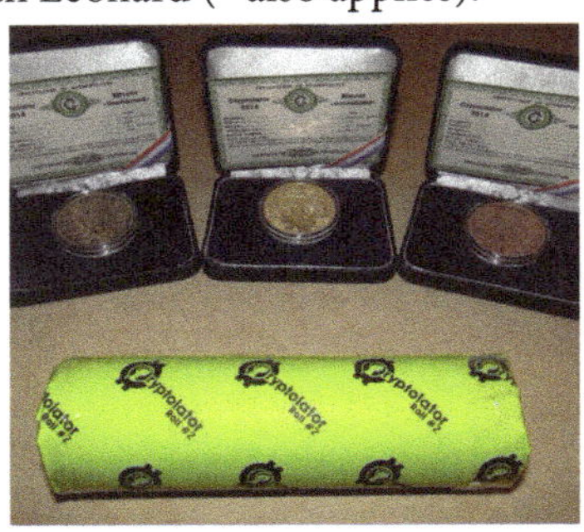

Image Credits (clockwise): Cryptolator (3), Elias Ahonen (1)

Cryptonic

Cryptonic is based in Latvia, and has made both Monero and Bitcoin themed coins. The producers have a very positive opinion of the crypto-currency Monero, after which most of their coins are themed. Monero was launched in April 2014 as 'BitMonero', but was later re-named as a matter of branding.

Cryptonic was already working with a jeweler on a Bitcoin round in February 2014, two months before Monero was released. After a second version of a wax model of the new coin had been created, production was ready to begin until the artist reported that the caster had gone on a holiday during which the wax prototype had been eaten by a mouse. With Monero being released around the same time that the design needed to be re-done, Cryptonic switched focus to the new crypto-currency.

A common theme in Cryptonic's Monero rounds is the use of Esperanto, which is a 'constructed language', with the purpose of providing a global language that is politically neutral, logical, and easy to learn. Quite interestingly, these ideals with the values of crypto-currency when considered from the perspective of money and trade as opposed to communication. The reason Esperanto is relevant to these coins is that 'Monero' is actually the word for 'currency' in Esperanto.

Cryptonic coins have a special element that makes them a little more than 'rounds', even though they are categorized as such. Through the website, holders of a physical coin can use the code that is engraved onto the side of the coin to 'bind' the coin to either a BTC, LTC, DOGE, or XMR address.

Image Credits: Cryptonic

Cryptonic

Monero Cryptocoin Silver

Manufacturer: Cryptonic
Year: 2014, 2015
Denomination: XMR
Type: Round

Version	Mintage
2014	31
2015	60
TOTAL	**91**

Material: .999 Silver
Diameter: 38 mm
Thickness: 3 mm
Weight: 33.8 g
Country: Latvia

'Sekura – Privata – Nespurebla' is written on the front rim of this round, which is Esperanto for 'Secure – Private –Untraceable'. A large Monero logo takes up the majority of the remaining space. The back reads 'Gi Estas Vera' meaning 'It is real'. The black and orange logo on the front of the coin is enamel, which has been used by other manufacturers such as Cryptogifts and even Casascius in the 25 BTC coin.

Image Credits (clockwise): Elias Ahonen (all)

Cryptonic

Monero Cryptocoin Plated

Manuf.	Cryptonic
Year	2014
Denom.	XMR
Type	Round
Mintage	100
Material	Silver Pl. Brass
Diameter	38mm
Thickness	3 mm
Weight	27 g
Country	Latvia

Monero is an alternative crypto-currency with significant fundamental differences to Bitcoin. Interestingly, 5 percent of all revenue from the sale of these rounds (and the pure silver Monero rounds) was donated to a Monero development fund. The front reads 'Vivu la Financa Libereco' which is Esperanto for 'Long Live Financial Freedom' and the back reads 'Cifereca Monero' which translates to 'Digital Currency'.

Image Credits (clockwise): Howard Kesselman (all)

Cryptonic

Bitcoin Cryptocoin

Manufacturer: Cryptonic
Year: 2014
Denomination: BTC
Type: Round

Version	Mintage
Silver Star	50
Gold Star	107
TOTAL	**157**

Material: Silver Pl. Brass
Diameter: 38 mm
Thickness: 3 mm
Weight: 28.3 g
Country: Latvia

This coin comes in all-silver or with gold plating over the 'Bitcoin star'. The back is the same design as other Cryptonic rounds. The front reads 'All Aboard – Mission to Cryptomars'. This 'Cryptomars' is likely a reference to the popular saying 'to the moon', which conveys that crypto-currency will eventually see an astronomical rise in value and relevance. It is probable that the star design on the coin is meant to add to this symbolism. The backside declares 'Cryptocoin Forever', flanked by infinity symbols on the left and right signifying the perpetual nature of crypto-currency.

Image Credits (clockwise): Howard Kesselman (all)

CryptoVault

CryptoVault put its first coins on sale in March of 2015, and is run by Kyle O'Brien, Jordan Parks, and Brett Lanning from Indiana. The idea was conceived in the very early days of physical Bitcoin in 2012, sprouting from a desire to create a "product that…everyone can use to safeguard their crypto-currencies".[1] Prior to launch, the founders attempted to raise $5,000 using the crowd-funding website startjoin.com, but only managed to see $220 in pre-orders and the campaign was canceled.

The idea behind CryptoVault is reflected in its name; a completely secure method of long-term storage for crypto-currencies. This coin is not intended or imagined to be used as a physical 'cash' version of crypto-currency, but a private 'vault'. Like many other 'DIY' type Bitcoin coins, the actual function of the coin is no different than that of a sealed paper wallet that can similarly be used to store the private keys to any amount or type of crypto-currency. The only difference is aesthetics; it looks nice and is a conversation piece. At the time of writing, the company has numerous other coins in the works.

Image Credits (clockwise): CryptoVault (all)

1. "About Us" Link: http://www.mycryptovault.net/pages/about-us

CryptoVault

Vault Coin

Manufacturer: CryptoVault
Year: 2014
Denomination: N/A
Type: DIY

Version	Mintage
Normal	497 *
Lim. Ed. 24K Gold Pl.	8
TOTAL	**505**

Material: Nickel Copper Alloy
Diameter: 33.3 mm
Thickness: 1.6 mm
Weight: 10.8 g
Country: USA

This coin is made of an alloy that is both strong and highly resistant to heat, with the design goal of protecting the private key even in the event of a fire. Although the current hologram is not sufficient to ensure protection in extreme situations, CryptoVault plans to design new holograms that will be fire, heat, and water resistant with some kind of tracking capability to prevent loss. Though 500 have been produced, it is not a hard limit and more may be minted at CryptoVault's discretion. The rare gold plated versions (shown on next page) are identical, and were originally made for the founders.

Image Credits (clockwise): CryptoVault, Howard Kesselman

CryptoVault

Lim. Ed. Silver Vault Coin

Manuf.	CryptoVault
Year	2015
Denom.	N/A
Type	DIY
Mintage	.999 Silver
Material	8
Diameter	33.3 mm
Thickness	1.6 mm
Weight	0.5 ozt
Country	USA

The rare silver coin is identical to the alloy round in all ways except its metal composition. The face of the round resembles a bank vault door, symbolizing the security 'vault' that it is meant to function as. It is surrounded by binary 1's and 0's to signify encryption security. Like the gold plated coin (pictured; upper right), this was originally made exclusively for the founders but a few were made available publicly.

Image Credits (clockwise): Howard Kesselman, CryptoVault (2)

CryptoVest

CryptoVest launched its first edition coins in September 2013, after a design contest was run on the Bitcointalk.org forum. The winning design was submitted by user 'Zinodaur', which became the namesake of the edition. CryptoVest itself is not solely a 'crypto-mint', but instead a sort of 'investment club' run from the UK. These coins were not created as a profit seeking venture, but as a form of advertising for the investment club and for crypto-currencies in general.

The coins received a very positive reception, and were distributed widely. Like Casascius, SerpCoin, and Microsoul, it is clear that CryptoVest were created out of enthusiasm and with a hobbyist approach, though the number of minted coins being 4,000, it was no small hobby.

As an added promotion, CryptoVest also had chocolate versions of the coins made, which were given out. Upon production of the chocolate coins, the owner of CryptoVest commented:

"I live in a college town, so I was thinking of going to a computer science building on campus and handing them out to a bunch of students. Meanwhile, introducing them to Litecoins and Bitcoins. Maybe this will introduce a couple new developers (or users) into the community, that wouldn't have otherwise learned about Bitcoin/Litecoin."[1]

A higher quality version of the coins with precision minting and high-security holograms was promised, but that expansion has been abandoned.

Below: The promotional chocolate coins (left), and the actual coins (right) before hologram application.

Image Credits (clockwise): CryptoVest (all)

1. "CryptoVest Physical Litecoins (Metal Alloy)- NEW: 'Special First Edition' Coins" Link: https://bitcointa.lk/threads/cryptovest-physical-litecoins-metal-alloy-new-special-first-edition-coins.165915/

CryptoVest

Zinodaur Physical Litecoin

Manufacturer: CryptoVest
Year: 2013
Denomination: 1 LTC
Type: UF, DIY

Version	Mintage
First Ed. (UF, DIY)	3,150
Special Ed. (UF)	850
TOTAL	**4,000**

Material: Zinc Alloy
Diameter: 39 mm
Thickness: 3.1 mm
Weight: 24.1 g
Country: USA

The imagery at the center of this coin represents Litecoin mining, security, speed (as compared to Bitcoin), and global applicability. The original intent was to release three distinct versions of the coin: an 'Economy', 'Executive', and even 'Chocolate'. While the first would be made cheaply, the second was to be made to the highest standards. The chocolate coins were a 'fun' addition, and used as a promotion. Due to a lack of demand, the 'Executive' version never materialized. A batch of 4,000 coins were produced, 850 of which were designated as 'Special First Edition' coins. These 'SFE' coins feature a 'window' in the hologram (pictured above), whereas the remaining 3,150 have no such window. The SFE coins were meant to be funded with 1 LTC prior to shipment, but the idea was abandoned due to the publicized legal complications faced by Casascius. The other coins (without hologram windows) were never meant to be pre-funded.

Image Credits (clockwise):Elias Ahonen, Howard Kesselman (1)

Denarium

Denarium is a business unit of Prasos Oy. A Bitcoin start-up based in Jyväskylä, Finland and is directed by CEO Henry Brade and his team. In addition to physical Bitcoins, they operate Finland's largest Bitcoin exchange (Bittiraha), a network of Bitcoin ATM's around the country (Bittimaatti), and an online store dedicated to Bitcoin related items (BTC Store). When considering them as a producer of physical Bitcoins, it is worth taking into account that the online store was once a primary re-seller of Casascius coins in Europe. With the introduction of their own coins, the reselling activities were however wound down. In early 2015, Prasos Oy sold about 8 percent of the company for 227,203 EUR (~250,000 USD) to 268 individual investors via crowd-fund investing site Invesdor.com.

The idea behind Denarium is to create cost effective physical Bitcoins with an appeal to worldwide clients, backed by the trusted Prasos Oy brand. A key difference between Denarium coins and those of most other manufacturers is their intentional simplicity. The coins are made in the same spirit as Casascius brass coins: they have the same material, same size, and a hologram that is at first glance identical to Casascius' with only a difference in brand name. It is a reasonable assumption that Denarium's intention is to begin where Casascius left off in distributing low-cost physical Bitcoins for purposes of education and recognition, as opposed to creating artistic pieces and curiosities to established collectors. While Denarium's market certainly includes collectors, the company's stated focus is on Asian markets which are quite ignored by other manufacturers. Prasos Oy is one of the few producers of physical Bitcoins which have other significant business interests unrelated to the coins they produce, and of those, Prasos Oy (via Bittiraha) arguably has the most trusted reputation.

Image Credits (clockwise): Denarium

Denarium

1/100 BTC

Manuf.	Denarium
Year	2015
Denom.	0.01 BTC
Type	PF, UF
Mintage	2,000
Material	Brass
Diameter	28.6 mm
Thickness	1.7 mm
Weight	7.65 g
Country	Finland

This coin features a fraction on the front to clearly demonstrate the denomination of the coin compared to a full bitcoin, with the same amount in 'bits' (one-millionths of a bitcoin).

The image on this coin is a dove, which symbolizes freedom. It is not the first time the theme has been used on a physical Bitcoin; a dove is the central theme in Recalescence Coins. The dove is meant to show that Bitcoin provides the user with unparalleled financial freedom, allowing money to be transferred freely in the same way in which a dove is free to fly the skies without restriction.

Image Credits (clockwise): Howard Kesselman (all)

Denarium

1/10 BTC

Manuf.	Denarium
Year	2015
Denom.	0.1 BTC
Type	PF, UF
Mintage	2,000
Material	Brass
Diameter	28.6 mm
Thickness	1.7 mm
Weight	7.65 g
Country	Finland

The hologram demands attention, as it is nearly identical to Casascius' Series 2 hologram. The only difference is the name of the brand (Denarium instead of Casascius), along with a different center design and 'Authentic' instead of 'Original' written in the upper band. The inspiration by Casascius and emulation is clear when comparing the holograms (see the Casascius hologram pictures on the bottom left). It should be noted that while the hologram window displays the first-bits as expected, the hologram itself is also engraved with a serial number starting with E (for 'Empty' unfunded 'UF') or L (for 'Loaded'; pre-funded 'PF').

The image on the coin is that of a bull, though it has received some criticism for not being obvious (for example, it has been initially interpreted to be an image of Italy). The bull is a symbol of economic prosperity and the increasing value of financial instruments, which makes it a fitting image to place on an asset such as Bitcoin which the holder expects to rise in value.

Image Credits (clockwise): Howard Kesselman (2), Andrew Dobbins

Denarium

Custom

Manuf.	Denarium
Year	2015
Denom.	BTC
Type	PF, UF
Mintage	2,000
Material	Brass
Diameter	28.6 mm
Thickness	1.7 mm
Weight	7.65 g
Country	Finland

The Denarium Custom coin has no stated face value, but instead comes unfunded or pre-funded according to customer preference with any amount between 0.01 BTC and 5 BTC. The design is simplistic and without imagery, in contrast with the other Denarium coins. The Bitcoin 'B' is on an angle, drawing similarities to the bhCoin hologram (compare to the small photo on the right). In addition to the 'B', the front contains the words 'Bitcoin - Denarium - 2015'.

Image Credits (clockwise): Denarium, Howard Kesselman

Finite By Design

Finite by Design LLC is one of the earlier producers of physical crypto-currency, with seven varieties of 1oz silver coins produced in 2013 themed after six different crypto-currencies. F*D (as it is commonly known) is run by Christopher Mrozek and is based in the USA. Christopher was the first to produce physical coins for a number of crypto-currencies such as Namecoin, Primecoin, and Cryptogenic Bullion. In fact, Finite by Design was the first mint to focus on creating coins of various crypto-currencies, and its scale and quality has not been matched to date with similarly minded producers such as Genesis.

The name 'Finite By Design' can be interpreted to refer to the way crypto-currencies like Bitcoin are designed to be finite in supply forever, unlike 'fiat' money which is not necessarily based on a finite resource and where supply can be increased by decision of the central issuer. Though physical coins have been F*D's main focus, it has also produced 'Crypto Cards' which are credit card sized plastic wallets. The silver coins have always been seen as highly premium products, with initial prices being $200 for a 1oz silver coin.

Below: (Left) a physical Peercoin in its presentation box, (right) an assortment of coins

Image Credits (clockwise): Finite By Design (all)

Finite By Design

1/10 Bitcoin Proof

Manuf.	F*D
Year	2013
Denom.	0.1 BTC
Type	UF
Mintage	50
Material	.999 Silver
Diameter	39 mm
Thickness	3 mm
Weight	1 ozt
Country	USA

This 0.1 BTC coin was released in the same year as the iconic Casascius 1 oz silver 1 BTC coin. It sets the tone for the early F*D coins, which are characterized as being of simple design while drawing attention to the currency symbol.

1 Litecoin Proof

Manuf.	F*D
Year	2013
Denom.	1 LTC
Type	UF
Mintage	50
Material	.999 Silver
Diameter	39 mm
Thickness	3 mm
Weight	1 ozt
Country	USA

This physical Litecoin was released in the same year as Lealana was started. With both Lealana and F*D using the same Litecoin 'L' design imposed over diagonal stripes, it became a standard for future physical Litecoins such as Coinographic. Compare to the image of a Lealana 10 LTC coin on the right. The back outer rim is made up of 21 stars, in reference to 21 million which is the maximum number of bitcoins that can ever be created.

Image Credits (clockwise): Howard Kesselman (4)

Finite By Design

Peercoin Proof

Manufacturer: F*D
Year: 2013
Denomination: 10 PPC
Type: UF

Version	Mintage
All Silver	50
Gold Rim	50
TOTAL	**100**

Material: .999 Silver
Diameter: 39 mm
Thickness: 3 mm
Weight: 1 ozt
Country: USA

Two types of this coin have been made; all-silver and with gold rimming. Peercoin is one of the early crypto-currencies, with some interesting differences to Bitcoin. These include no fixed limit on the number of possible PPC in existence, and it is designed to attain a 1 percent annual rate of inflation. The hologram for this coin is notably very small. In 2013, the BTC value of the 10 PPC face value varied between 0.11 BTC and 0.15 BTC.

Primecoin Proof

Manuf.	F*D
Year	2013
Denom.	11 XPM
Type	UF
Mintage	100*
Material	.999 Silver
Diameter	39 mm
Thickness	3 mm
Weight	1 ozt
Country	USA
*Two batches of 50 coins	

Both the front and the hologram feature the Primecoin logo. Primecoin is an early crypto-currency designed by Sunny King (a pseudonym for an anonymous individual or group) who also had a hand in Peercoin. Unlike Bitcoin miners which use vast amounts of electricity in their quest to 'win' hashing contests and thus create new blocks, the goal of Primecoin's mining process is to discover long chains of prime numbers which are useful in a number of mathematical calculations. As a tribute to this, the face value is 11 which is a prime number.

Image Credits (clockwise): Howard Kesselman (2), Finite By Design (2)

Finite By Design

10 Namecoins Proof

Manuf.	F*D
Year	2013
Denom.	10 NMC
Type	UF
Mintage	50
Material	.999 Silver
Diameter	39 mm
Thickness	3 mm
Weight	1 ozt
Country	USA

This coin is designed to store Namecoin, which is the first 'fork' of Bitcoin created in April 2011. This 'clone' was modified slightly to have some unique uses, including a potential for the Namecoin infrastructure to be used in the running of a censorship-resistant '.bit' domain. In 2013, the BTC value of the 10 NMC face value varied between 0.1 BTC and 0.016 BTC.

Cryptogenic Bullion Proof

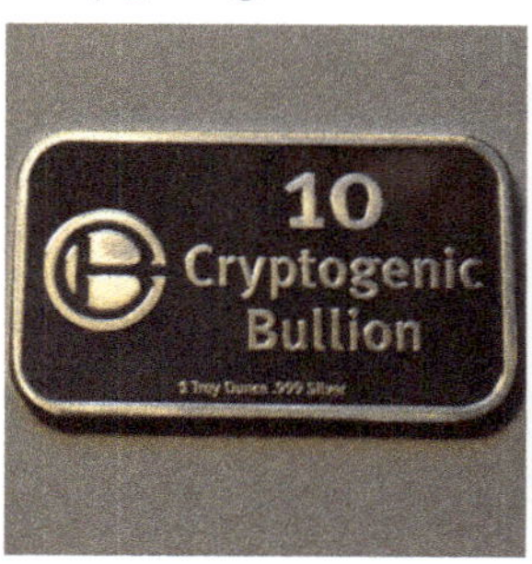

Manuf.	F*D
Year	2013
Denom.	10 CBX
Type	UF
Mintage	50
Material	.999 Silver
Diameter	50 x 29 mm
Thickness	2 mm
Weight	1 ozt
Country	USA

This is the first physical crypto-currency in a silver bar form and second implementation of a 'bar' after Casascius' various brass bars. 'Cryptogenic Bullion' obviously draws parallels to precious metal bullion, making a silver bar (which arguably conveys the idea of 'bullion' better than a silver coin or round), a natural choice to store the crypto-currency. In mid-2013, Cryptogenic Bullion was re-branded to Crypto Bullion. In 2013, the BTC value of the 10 CBX face value varied between 0.008 BTC and 0.04 BTC.

Image Credits (clockwise): Finite By Design (2), Elias Ahonen (2)

Finite By Design

Doge Proof (Antique Nickel)

Manuf.	F*D
Year	2014
Denom.	DOGE
Type	DIY
Mintage	100
Material	Nickel
Diameter	39 mm
Thickness	2 mm
Weight	26.2 g
Country	USA

These Dogecoin themed DIY rounds were released in the same year as some other physical DOGE coins and rounds including Crypto Imperator and Shibemint. These coins have a different style compared to either of the other mints and the nickel coin is the first Doge themed coin to be made with that metal. It should be noted that these coins do not have a denomination, with the buyer being free to load them with any amount they wish.

Doge Proof (Antique Copper)

Compare this design to the image of Shibemint copper Doge round on the right. The Finite By Design coin has more detail, while the Shibemint round (Pictured on left) has a smoother and 'cleaner' appearance. Like many other F*D coins, the outer back side has a ring of stars, with the standard Finite By Design hologram in the middle.

Manuf.	F*D
Year	2014
Denom.	DOGE
Type	DIY
Mintage	100
Material	Copper
Diameter	39 mm
Thickness	2 mm
Weight	27 g
Country	USA

Image Credits (clockwise): Howard Kesselman (3), Elias Ahonen (1)

Finite By Design

Darkcoin Proof

Manuf.	F*D
Year	2015
Denom.	DRK
Type	DIY
Mintage	100
Material	Ant. Silver
Diameter	39 mm
Thickness	2 mm
Weight	26 g
Country	USA

This coin is made to hold Darkcoin, which was later renamed 'Dash' to remove negative connotations of the word 'dark', and to combine the words 'digital' and 'cash'. The word 'Dash' also implies speed. The currency uses a system called 'Darksend' which 'anonymizes' transactions, unlike those made with Bitcoin which are stored forever on a public ledger. The 'D' logo on the coin is the old version; a new logo was made to accompany the new name.

Ether Proof

Manuf.	F*D
Year	2015
Denom.	ETH
Type	DIY
Mintage	100
Material	Brass
Diameter	39 mm
Thickness	2 mm
Weight	27 g
Country	USA

Ether is a notable crypto-currency, in that it is often considered as a 'next generation' crypto-currency or 'Bitcoin 2.0'. Ethereum is unlike most other crypto-currencies, and there is wide interest in following its progress from both Bitcoin enthusiasts and from outside industry. The overall goal of the Ethereum 'project' is to develop infrastructure that is capable of fully decentralizing the Internet. Finite By Design is a proponent of Ethereum, and has committed to producing several Ether-themed bars in addition to this coin.

Image Credits (clockwise): Howard Kesselman (all)

Finite By Design

Real Bitcoin Proof

Manuf.	F*D
Year	2015
Denom.	BTC
Type	DIY
Mintage	100
Material	Ant. Gold
Diameter	39 mm
Thickness	2 mm
Weight	26g
Country	USA

This coin could very well be seen as the epitome of a 'classic' physical Bitcoin due to its tasteful simplicity. Strikingly, the front is virtually identical to the early 'CoinedBits' round released in 2011 (compare small photo on the right), with the raised outer rim being the only discernible difference. The coin contains a central Bitcoin 'B', the word 'Bitcoin', and the common motto 'Vires In Numeris'. The back contains words and phrases relating to Bitcoin: " 'The Real Bitcoin' | Series 1 | 2015 | Peer-to-Peer Technology | Decentralized Trust | Satoshi Nakamoto".

Image Credits (clockwise): Howard Kesselman (2), Coinedbits

Finite By Design

5" Bitcoin Bar

Like the 'Real Bitcoin' coin, this bar has a simple and classic design. It features two crossed hammers around the Bitcoin 'B', which symbolize bitcoin mining. The English version of the Bitcoin motto 'Strength In Numbers' is prominent on the bar, and the hologram and private key is at the bottom. The back of the bar simply has the word 'Bitcoin' written diagonally across it in repetitive fashion, in a similar way as some gold and silver bullion mints have been known to do with their own brand name. This bar perhaps best re-creates the purpose and theme of the original Casascius brass storage bars with its high quality, timeless mass appeal, and simple function and design.

Manuf.	F*D
Year	2015
Denom.	BTC
Type	DIY
Mintage	100
Material	Copper & Brass Alloy
Diameter	111 x 57 mm
Thickness	6.35 mm
Weight	192 g
Country	USA

Image Credits (clockwise): Howard Kesselman (all)

Finite By Design

5" 'Ethereum Frontier' Ether Bar (Antique Gold)

Manuf.	F*D
Year	2015
Denom.	ETH
Type	DIY
Mintage	100
Material	Copper & Brass Alloy
Diameter	111 x 57 mm
Thickness	6.35 mm
Weight	192 g
Country	USA

The theme of this design is 'Frontier' which said to be the first of four stages in the launch process of the Ethereum network. The crypto-currency 'Ether' is often imagined as the 'crypto-fuel' of the Ethereum network, which explains why the words 'pure cryptofuel' are written below the Ethereum logo on these bars. The back of the bar displays an outer-space scene where a landing vehicle is about to touch down on a celestial object. The theme of 'crypto fuel' is apparent here (think 'rocket fuel', 'to the moon', etc), and the new world appears to be declared as being the 'Frontier' in large letters.

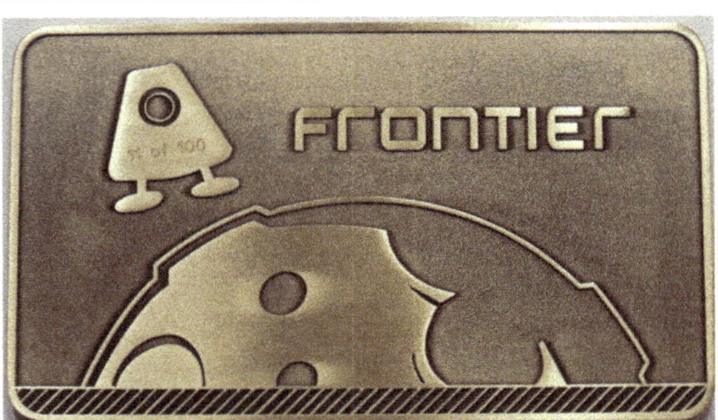

Image Credits (clockwise): Howard Kesselman (all)

Finite By Design

5" 'Ethereum Frontier' Ether Bar (Antique Copper)

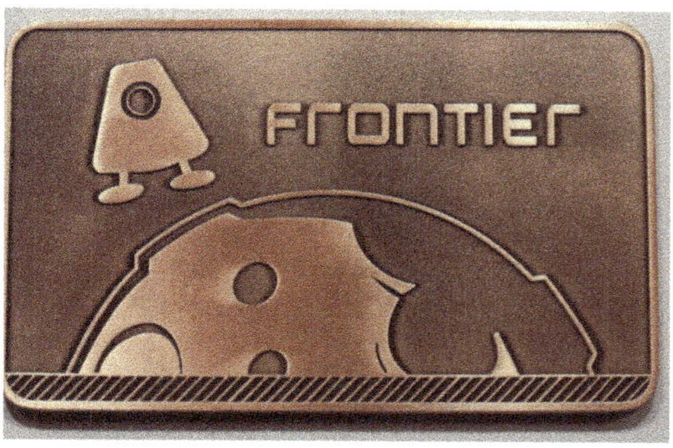

5" 'Ethereum Frontier' Ether Bar (Antique Silver)

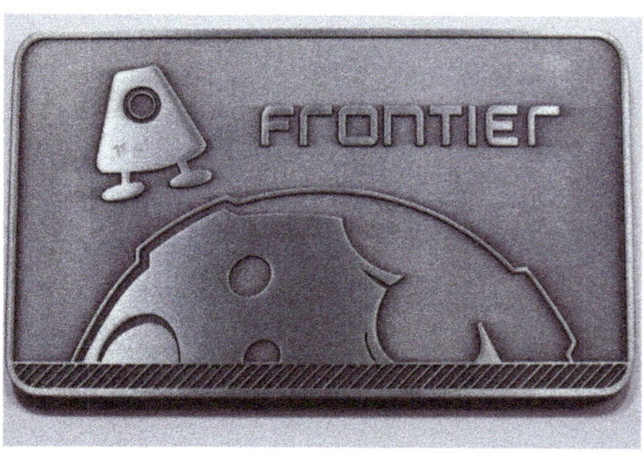

Manuf.	F*D
Year	2015
Denom.	ETH
Type	DIY
Mintage	100
Material	Copper & Brass Alloy
Diameter	111 x 57 mm
Thickness	6.35 mm
Weight	192 g
Country	USA

The size of these bars should not be ignored. They are significantly larger and heavier than the Casascius bearer bars, which are the second largest bars designed to store crypto-currency. The Casascius bars weigh only 118 g, have a diameter of 80 mm x 40 mm, and a thickness of 6 mm meaning they are smaller by all measurements.

Manuf.	F*D
Year	2015
Denom.	ETH
Type	DIY
Mintage	100
Material	Copper & Brass Alloy
Diameter	111 x 57 mm
Thickness	6.35 mm
Weight	192 g
Country	USA

Image Credits (clockwise): Howard Kesselman (all)

Geek Bitcoin

5 mbtc

Manuf.	Geek Bitcoin
Year	2014
Denom.	0.005 BTC
Type	UF, DIY
Mintage	
Material	Gold Pl. Brass
Diameter	25 mm
Thickness	1.5 mm
Weight	6 g
Country	China

This physical Bitcoin bears the phrase 'In Bitcoin We Trust'. Its face has the Bitcoin 'B', along with the denomination of five mBTC and a constellation of five stars to symbolize the denomination. The outer rim of the front has a star on each side, which is rather common considering the same theme is used by CoinedBits and Finite By Design. The back consists of a custom hologram putting heavy emphasis on the Bitcoin logo, as is quite common. Perhaps most notably, Geek Bitcoin is based in China. Though some coins have been manufactured there, this is the first original coin of this type sold from China.

Image Credits (clockwise): Howard Kesselman (all)

Genesis

Genesis coins were inspired by the creator's observation that there were not very many physical coins available for holding crypto-currencies other than Bitcoin, Litecoin, and Dogecoin. To fill this need, a 'generic' coin was created to represent a dozen different crypto-currencies. Each coin contains a private key for a single crypto-currency. Both the specific crypto-currency and the public key is engraved on the coin. This method of differentiating the coins was chosen instead of minting several small lots of coins due to the impractically high cost of the latter.

Genesis coins commemorate the 'Genesis Blocks' of the crypto-currencies they represent. In crypto-currency, a 'Genesis Block' refers to the first 'block' in the blockchain upon which the currency is based. The 'mining' of this block can be seen as the official 'launch' of a crypto-currency, and is thus a highly significant event.

Genesis' distribution model is unique, and is inspired by baseball cards. The majority (about two thirds) of the coins are bought blindly as 'packs'. These packs are sealed plastic pouches which look identical, meaning that the coin that the buyer receives is random (just like when buying a pack of trading cards). The remaining third of coins were offered for direct (non-random) sale. The model of blind distribution caused interesting results, because there was great variability in the 'rareness' and desirability of the coins. Of 300 coins in the first series, 120 were considered 'premium' (gold-plated and numbered 1-10 for each of the 10 featured currencies). Of these 120 premium coins, 30 were considered highly desirable due to being made for more mainstream crypto-currencies. The effect that this caused was indeed very similar to that which is commonly observed in baseball card collectors, who are willing to buy large numbers of less desirable cards in the hopes of getting lucky with a rare and valuable card. It is worth asking if Genesis would have been nearly as successful if a traditional distribution model was employed, considering that many collectors are not particularly interested in less popular crypto-currencies.

Image Credits: bitcointalk.org user 'CJBianco'

Genesis

Gold Plated (various)

This gold-plated coin is surrounded by the names of twelve crypto-currencies, with the name of each of them etched onto the front. There are also twelve dates on the coin; corresponding to the dates of the 'Genesis Block' of each crypto-currency (This refers to the first 'mined' block of coins; essentially the 'launch' date). Though there are 120 of the identically minted coins, they are sub-divided into twelve distinct categories of ten each. These categories are the different crypto-currencies for which the coin functions as a wallet. Each coin has a private key under a secure hologram, with the public key engraved on the coin itself. This public key (and hidden private key) works only with the crypto-currency whose name is engraved on the front of the coin. Exactly 10 of these coins exist for each of the following crypto-currencies: Bitcoin, Litecoin, Dogecoin, Clams, Coin2, Darkcoin, DNotes, Hyper, Namecoin, Peercoin, Reddcoin, and ShadowCash.

Manuf.	Genesis
Year	2015
Denom.	Various
Type	UF
Mintage	120
Material	Copper / Brass Alloy
Diameter	38 mm
Thickness	3 mm
Weight	27.8 g
Country	USA

Image Credits (clockwise): bitcointalk.org user 'snarlpill', Howard Kesselman, bitcointalk.org user 'snarlpill'

Genesis

Silver Plated (various)

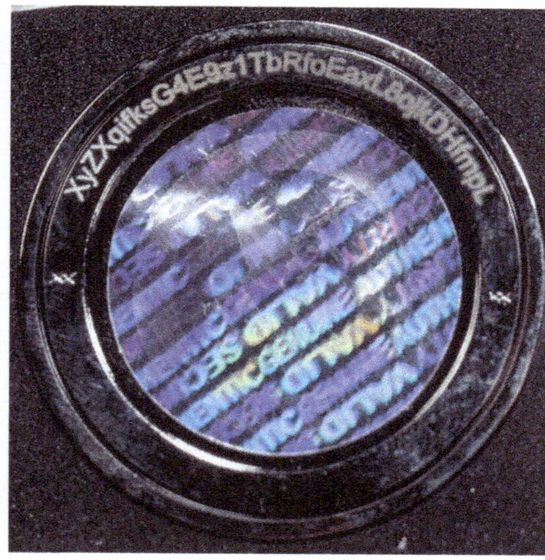

Manuf.	Genesis
Year	2015
Denom.	Various
Type	UF
Mintage	180
Material	Copper / Brass Alloy
Diameter	38 mm
Thickness	3 mm
Weight	27.8 g
Country	USA

This silver-plated coin has the same concept as the gold-plated coin, though it is designed to be the less valuable Genesis coin as evidenced by mintage numbers and the color (with silver being perceived as less valuable compared to gold). Instead of being available in twelve different crypto-currencies like the gold-plated version, it is available in nine crypto-currencies with 20 coins of each style. The nine crypto-currencies are: Clams, Coin2, Darkcoin, DNotes, Hyper, Namecoin, Peercoin, Reddcoin, and ShadowCash. It is notable that Bitcoin, Litecoin, and Dogecoin are missing. Leaving out the three most popular crypto-currencies in this silver-plated edition is done to make them more sought after, effectively meaning that there are only 30 'highly desirable' coins out of the 300 Genesis coins in the first series. This 'engineered rarity' drove the re-sale value of Bitcoin, Litecoin, and Dogecoin Genesis coins up, encouraging collectors to buy Genesis coins almost as if it were a lottery. There are three documented errors: Bitcoin #2, Coin2 #2, and Peercoin #9 all have their currency name and serial number printed upside-down. Additionally, 'ShadowCash' is mistakenly spelled as 'Shadowcoin'.

Image Credits (clockwise): Howard Kesselman (all)

∞ Infinitum Bitcoins

Infinitum Bitcoins

Infinitum Bitcoins is based in the British Virgin Islands, and has so far produced 1 oz and 2 oz fine silver coins as part of the 'Ingenium' series. 'Ingenium' is Latin for 'genius', which is fitting considering that the coins feature images of Leonardo Da Vinci and Albert Einstein who are perhaps the most well-known embodiments of the word. Of course, the general idea of the series is to assert that the concept of Bitcoin is itself a work of genius, and would deserve great respect from (and can thus be associated with) some of history's most well regarded minds. Contenders for future coins in the series have been said to include Michelangelo, Archimedes, and Thomas Edison.

As evidenced by the superior quality, very large mintage numbers (over 3,200 2 oz silver coins), and professional marketing, Infinitum Bitcoins is a highly significant and prestigious manufacturer of physical Bitcoins. As a business, Infinitum is most closely comparable to Titan Bitcoin (in scale and investment) and Alitin Mint (in the similarity of coins and theme, especially regarding 2 oz silver coins dedicated to historical figures). Infinitum is a serious business venture; the production of Infinitum's inventory alone requiring well above $150,000 which would be out of reach for the majority of enthusiasts.

In the same way as Cryptolator, Infinitum coins are sold in three types: pre-funded/empty, DIY, and 2-factor.

Image Credits: Infinitum Bitcoins

Infinitum Bitcoins

Da Vinci 2015 2 Troy Oz Silver Bitcoin

Manuf.	Infinitum Bitcoins
Year	2015
Denom.	BTC
Type	UF, DIY
Mintage	2222
Material	.999 Silver
Diameter	50 mm
Thickness	3 mm
Weight	2 ozt
Country	BVI

This design style is inspired by ancient Roman coins, which often featured carved portrait-like images. Infinitum states "Da Vinci staring forward in deep gaze, contemplating the environment, observing his surroundings, questioning everything". The backside contains the phrase

"Actus Genio Sunt, Illi in Nulla re Tempus", which is Latin for "Acts of Genius are Never Lost in Time". This refers to Bitcoin, with the message being that Bitcoin is a work of genius that will endure long into the future. The hologram replaces first-bits with a QR code. It does not come with any BTC.

Image Credits (clockwise): Howard Kesselman (all)

Infinitum Bitcoins

Albert Einstein 2015 1 Troy Oz Silver One Bitcoin Cent

Manuf.	Infinitum Bitcoins
Year	2015
Denom.	0.01 BTC
Type	PF, DIY
Mintage	999
Material	.999 Silver
Diameter	40 mm
Thickness	3 mm
Weight	1 ozt
Country	BVI

In the same style as the Da Vinci coin, this coin has 'Albert Einstein 1879 – 1955' written beside an image of the genius. The backside contains a quote by Einstein which was selected for the coin to convey the perfection of the math behind Bitcoin: "Pure mathematics is, in its way, the poetry of logical ideas". Under the hologram, is the classic Bitcoin 'B' symbol, which is interestingly placed in the private key pit. The surface is filled with the word 'BITCOIN', creating additional friction which would make fraudulently removing the hologram more difficult than if it were a smooth surface.

Image Credits (clockwise): Howard Kesselman (all)

Infinitum Bitcoins

Nikola Tesla 2015 1 Troy Oz Silver Bitcoin

Manuf.	Infinitum Bitcoins
Year	2016
Denom.	0.01 BTC
Type	UF, DIY
Mintage	999
Material	.999 Silver
Diameter	40 mm
Thickness	3 mm
Weight	1 ozt
Country	BVI

This coin is an identical size and format as the Albert Einstein coin. The front has an image of Nikola Tesla, along with the years of his birth and death. The back is engraved with "If you only knew the magnificence of the 3, 6 and 9 then you would have the key to the universe", one of Tesla's famous quotes. While the quote is rather cryptic and mysterious, it could possibly be interpreted (even if not accurately) as something relevant to cryptology considering that it refers to numbers as being the 'key' to unlock something. Like on the Einstein coin, the space on which the hologram is set is detailed.

Image Credits (clockwise): Howard Kesselman, Infinitum Bitcoins

Infinitum Bitcoins

William Shakespeare 2015 1 Troy Oz Silver Bitcoin

Manuf.	Infinitum Bitcoins
Year	2016
Denom.	0.01 BTC
Type	UF, DIY
Mintage	999
Material	.999 Silver
Diameter	40 mm
Thickness	3 mm
Weight	1 ozt
Country	BVI

Like the two other coins belonging to the same format, this coin is denominated as 'One Bitcoin Cent', a unit more commonly known as a bitcent. The front has an image of English playwright William Shakespeare along with '1564 – 1616'. Shakespeare's famous quote "To be, or not to be, that is the question" is found on the back, along with the disclaimer 'Not Legal Tender of Any Government' which is on the back of all Infinitum coins.

Image Credits (clockwise): Howard Kesselman (all)

Jinn Bitcoin

Jinn Physical Bitcoin

Manuf.	Jinn
Year	2014
Denom.	1 BTC
Type	PF, UF
Mintage	100
Material	Silver Pl. Brass
Diameter	24 mm
Thickness	1 mm
Weight	8 g
Country	USA

Jinn Bitcoins coins were created by Kyle Hagin, as a crowd-funder 'prize' for anyone donating 100 USD or more to his project. The project in question was a 'Jinn e-wallet', for which he was seeking 10,000 USD in funding. This 'e-wallet' was to be a hand-held device connecting to various crypto-currency networks through a private cellular connection. The project did not receive sufficient funding, and the coins were offloaded to buyers on eBay.

The front of the coin is very similar in style and color to the Casascius Aluminum coins. Above the Bitcoin 'B', is the Latin phrase 'Societati Liberi' which means 'Free Society'. The word 'Jinn' is also on the front, along with '2014' and 'One Bitcoin'. The backside consists of a custom hologram featuring the Bitcoin 'B'.

Image Credits (clockwise): Howard Kesselman (all)

Jose Rodriguez

1 oz StartCOIN Mexican Silver coin

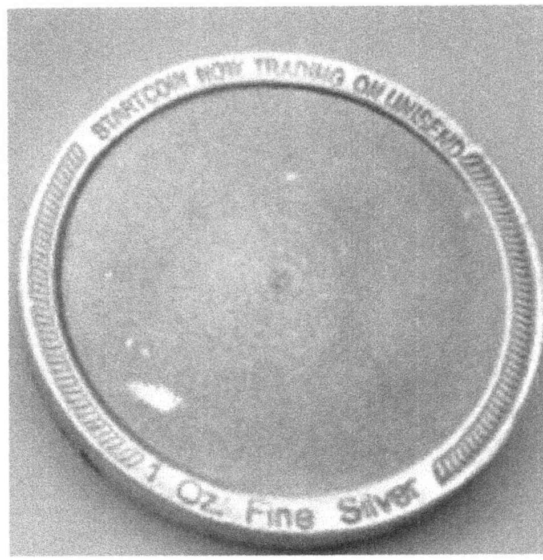

Manuf.	Jose Rodriguez
Year	2016
Denom.	500 START
Type	PF
Mintage	183*
Material	.999 Silver
Diameter	39 mm
Thickness	3 mm
Weight	1 oz
Country	Mexico

*Number reflects pre-orders; mintage number unknown.

These coins were minted by Jose Rodriguez in honor of Anarchapulco 2015, an anarcho-capitalist conference held in Acapulco, Mexico in February 2016.

Besides the year, the front features a prominent image of Guerrero Aguila, an Aztec warrior, as a symbol of strength and independence. There is also an anarchy themed 'A' logo for the Anarchapulco conference. In addition to the conference, the coin celebrates the integration of the alternative crypto-currency StartCOIN by Unisend, which is a Latin American Crypto-Currency exchange service. The back has space for a hologram, as well as the inscription 'StartCoin Now Trading on Unisend' and '1 Oz. Fine Silver'.

The coin is the result of a crowd-funding campaign on the website StartJOIN, where it successfully raised 11,440 USD to manufacture 183 coins.

Image Credits (clockwise): Jose Rodriguez (all)

Kialara

Kialara is a 'signature series' of complex physical Bitcoins created by artist Maxfield Wyatt Mellenbruch. While they consist of a coin with a private key hidden under a hologram, they have little else in common with the common physical crypto-currency format. One inherent danger with the hologram system is that it may technically be possible to inject a special chemical underneath the hologram allowing it to be temporarily removed by gentle peeling, leaving no obvious physical sign of doing so. This is no concern for Kialara coins, as the edges of the hologram are rendered inaccessible by a piece of metal bolted with specially treated screws. The head of each screw is drilled smooth to disallow unscrewing, and the bolts are treated with a special adhesive called Loctite RED which makes undoing them impossible unless heated to over 500 degrees Fahrenheit. This means that to access the private key, the hologram must be cut or torn instead of peeled. In addition, there is still an added layer of security: the entire coin is encased in a metal and glass holder, which has no way of being opened without violently smashing the glass. As for the private key, a special coating protects it against damage from any light, water, and gases. A Kialara physical Bitcoin is made to endure for generations. While these pieces are certainly functional wallets, their primary purpose is artistic. Mr. Mellenbruch considers the public and private keys to be a unique 'medium' in his art.

With Kialara, Max collaborated with HAVEN, an initiative that builds 'functioning beehive sculptures' in urban areas to provide wild honeybees with a safe sanctuary. Donating 10 USD per order to the project, he raised 4,750 USD in just a few months.

Image Credits (clockwise): Kialara (2), Howard Kesselman

Kialara

2014 Original

The original Kialara coin is made of aluminum. The front has a decorative design of two lion-like creatures and a dragon holding up the Bitcoin in the center. The creatures are made with several overlapping pieces and are three dimensional as a result. Max arrived at the design after studying various European coats-of-arms. The small Bitcoin in the center is made of aluminum, and is purely decorative. Though it would be classified as a round on its own, it forms part of the Kialara coin in which it is held. The red tab on the bottom says 'Remove When Funded' and is there to make it clear that there is no balance.

Manuf.	Kialara
Year	2014
Denom.	0.1 BTC
Type	UF
Mintage	2,500
Material	Aluminum
Diameter	93 x 56 mm
Thickness	8 mm
Weight	92 g
Country	USA

Image Credits (clockwise): Howard Kesselman (all)

Kialara

2015 1 BTC Original

These Kialara's are made of stainless steel instead of aluminum, and are much heavier as a result. They come in two versions, with the differentiating factor being the metal composition of the small bitcoin 'round' within the coin; .999 Silver or .999 Gold. All Kialara coins are serialized, with the serial number engraved on the coin, visible through the hologram. The year is displayed in the same way. An interesting fact about Kialara coins is that in 2015, one of them was gifted to Sir Richard Branson by Matthew Roszak, who is a producer of *The Rise and Rise of Bitcoin* documentary.

Manufacturer: Kialara
Year: 2015
Denomination: 1 BTC
Type: UF

Sub-Type	Mintage
Silver	250
Gold	100
Total	**350**

Material: Stainless Steel
Diameter: 93 x 56 mm
Thickness: 8 mm
Weight: 183 g
Country: USA

Image Credits (clockwise): Kialara, Elias Ahonen

Kialara

2015 Labyrinth

The Kialara Labyrinth coins are perhaps the first interactive physical bitcoins. While the hologram and private key are on one side as usual, the other side has a labyrinth game that can be played by tilting the coin to control the bearings inside. The coin comes in two versions; one with ceramic bearings and another with pure .999 Silver bearings. These coins can be distinguished from the other side by virtue of the red surface on which the public key is written. They are denominated as '100,000 bits', which is equal to 0.1 BTC. One bit is equal to 100 Satoshi.

Manufacturer: Kialara
Year: 2015
Denomination: 0.1 BTC
Type: UF

Sub-Type	Mintage
Ceramic Bear.	1,800
Silver Bear.	700
Total	**2,500**

Material: Stainless Steel
Diameter: 93 x 56 mm
Thickness: 8 mm
Weight: 97 g
Country: USA

Image Credits (clockwise): Howard Kesselman (all)

Kialara

Excavatorelevator 1

This coin is something special, along with the other one in this style. It is a print of an abstract piece visualizing the concept of 'blockchain' by Ricky Allman. The coin itself is 1 ounce of silver, and can be removed from its casing with the loosening of two screws. The hidden side of the coin is blank, and the buyer can affix one of the included holograms to it along with a custom private key. The visible side of the coin simply states 'Ricky Allman 2015', and the side is stamped with '.999 Fine Silver'. The inside of the casing (the back of the print) is signed and numbered. It is intriguing to note that the main focus of the 'coin' is its display case.

Manuf.	Kialara
Year	2015
Denom.	BTC
Type	DIY
Mintage	500
Material	.999 Silver
Diameter	93 x 56 mm
Thickness	8 mm
Weight	217 g
Country	USA

Image Credits (clockwise): Howard Kesselman (all)

Kialara

Current

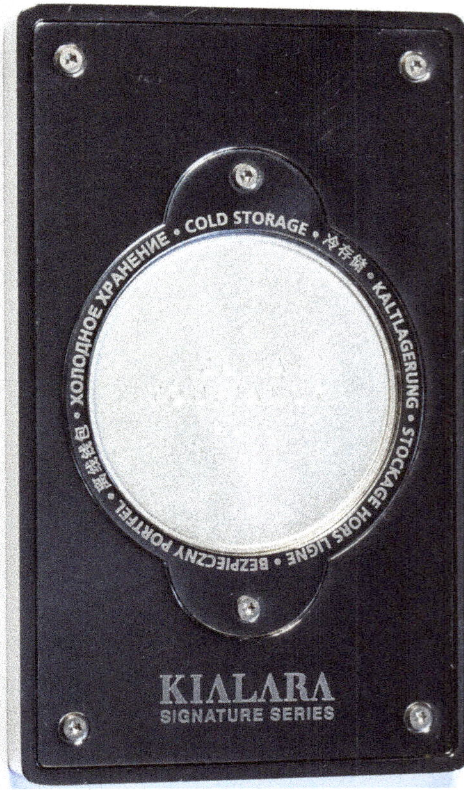

Following Excavatorelevator 1's format, this piece is artist Julia Tourianski's vision of Bitcoin. It is inspired by Théodore Géricault's The Raft of the Medusa, and each animal on the raft symbolizes an aspect of Bitcoin's current situation as follows: Platypus (unexpected), Bat (unprecedented), Giant Squid (doubted), Rats (global), Snow Leopard (hunted), Bear (prodigious), Hyena (stands up to the king), Wolf (misunderstood), Dingo (competitive), Bull (controversial), Albatross (ambitious), Lobster (potentially immortal), and Rhino (uncertainty). With all this on board, Julia remarked that "hopefully the raft will not sink, eh."[1]

Manuf.	Kialara
Year	2015
Denom.	BTC
Type	DIY
Mintage	500
Material	.999 Silver
Diameter	93 x 56 mm
Thickness	8 mm
Weight	217 g
Country	USA

Image Credits (clockwise): Howard Kesselman (all)

1. "Kialara Signature Series ~ Bitcoin Wallet" Link: https://imgur.com/a/RILhF

Lealana

Announced in June 2013 as 'Lealana Physical Litecoins', Lealana entered the market as a friendly competitor to Casascius focusing on Litecoin, the second most popular crypto-currency at the time. In the following months, coin offerings were expanded to offer both .999 Silver Litecoins and Bitcoins. A cheaper 0.1 BTC coin made of brass was also added, directly mimicking the composition and size of Casascius 1 BTC coins. Lealana coins are widely considered as being second to Casascius in both popularity and production quantity.

Lealana LLC is based in Hawaii and run by Noah Luis, better known by his handle 'smoothie' on the Bitcointalk.org and Litecointalk.org online forums where a majority of release announcements and customer interaction occurs. The brand has a Hawaiian inspiration, with later coins featuring Hawaiian-style artwork on both the hologram and face, along with a Hawaiian translation of the 'Strength in Numbers' motto popularized by Casascius.

Due to regulatory concerns similar to those faced by Casascius, Lealana paused sales for a period. In May 2014, sales resumed under a renewed framework of 'buyer-funded' coins. Under this new business model, coins were sold unfunded with a clearly visible 'BUYER FUNDED' printed onto the hologram. These buyer funded coins were delivered to the buyer with no crypto-currency balance, and they are rarely funded at all. As this change was made, Lealana changed the appearance of all coins by printing the first-bits address in green type instead of the normal black. This means that any coins with black text can be seen as the 'original' Lealana coins.

A method was devised to allow Lealana to ship pre-funded coins without the 'BUYER FUNDED' marking, while also avoiding any trouble with the established money-transmitting laws. This system required buyers to send the correct amount of BTC or LTC directly to the public key of each individual coin before being shipped out by Lealana once all coins were confirmed to be funded (and Lealana has been directly paid for the 'empty' coins). From a legal standpoint, Lealana is only producing and selling 'collectible tokens', while still being able to guarantee that these coins are fully funded to their stated denomination. This method could be aptly called 'supervised funding'.

Image Credits: Lealana

Lealana: the silver to Casascius' gold?

'Litecoin is the silver to Bitcoin's gold' has for long been a popular saying amongst Litecoin users. It conveys that while bitcoin will in their view remain as the most valuable digital store of value, they see litecoin as a more practical currency for everyday transactions. This is due to three principal factors. First, '1 LTC' would always be a considerably smaller and more useful amount than '1 BTC', which many foresee surpassing 10,000 USD (and some individuals even believe in a 1 million USD valuation in a 'global currency' scenario). Second, the Litecoin network is designed in such a way that it allows for more rapid confirmations of transactions and is often seen as being more scalable as a result. Thirdly, Litecoins are more efficient and cheaper to transact, because the algorithm is designed such that less energy is expended in the mining process (hence 'lite' in the name). All of these factors are actually very similar reasons by which silver is generally considered the secondary precious metal after gold. The fact that the Litecoin logo is silver while the logo for Bitcoin is gold or orange certainly does no disservice to this theory.

This idea of silver and gold becomes interesting when applied to Lealana and Casascius coins. Lealana was founded as a 'litecoin alternative' of Casascius physical Bitcoins; to create physical Litecoins for Litecoin users just like Casascius made Bitcoin 'real' and tangible to many. While the majority of Casascius' sales and auctions took place on the Bitcointalk forum, the majority of Lealana's initial sales were conducted on the similarly named but unaffiliated Litecointalk forum. Litecoin, which was originally founded as an alternative to Bitcoin, gained a popular 'physical form' through Lealana just as Bitcoin did from Casascius.

The value of Lealana and Casascius coins is another relevant aspect of this comparison, both in regards to face value and market value. The majority of Lealana litecoins have a low face value compared to Casascius coins, due to the exchange rate between LTC and BTC. Even the 25 LTC coin would have been worth a maximum of only 0.75 BTC at litecoin's peak in December 2013 (higher face-value Lealana coins arrived when Lealana physical Bitcoins were released, but their numbers were quite low). In comparison, the vast majority of Casascius coins have a face value of 1 BTC, with market values (for ungraded specimens) for such coins ranging from 1.2 BTC to 4 BTC depending on the coin. The market values for Lealana coins are much lower, making them more affordable to collectors and enthusiasts.

Although Casascius coins were produced in similar amounts as Lealana coins, sales for the latter take place much more frequently on eBay and the Bitcointalk forum, which are the primary marketplaces for physical crypto-currencies. This is because they are often easier to sell, while the potential buyer pool for Casascius coins remains quite small in comparison due to the high costs involved, as well additional expenses such as extra shipping insurance and escrow fees. Still, it is much simpler to sell a single Casascius coin for a significant amount, as opposed to selling a large number of Lealana coins (or any other similar coins).

Like Litecoin from Bitcoin, individual Lealana coins are directly inspired by Casascius coins. Prime examples include the Lealana 25 LTC coin, 1 BTC coin, and 0.1 BTC coin derived from the Casascius 25 BTC, Silver 1 BTC, and Brass 1 BTC coins respectively. Each of these except perhaps the 1 BTC coins is essentially a low-cost version derived from the corresponding Casascius coin.

With all this in mind, the idea that Lealana is to Casascius as silver is to gold is supported. This idea fits very well with the popular narrative of Litecoin being the silver to the gold that is Bitcoin. At this time, Casascius and Lealana coins dominate the physical crypto-coin market. They aren't just highly recognizable and traded at a higher frequency and value than coins by other manufacturers; they have the most established resale market (and predictable market value based on sub-type and condition).

Categorization

Lealana coins are divided into three distinct sub-types which correspond to different periods of production and changes in the process that resulted in visible differences in the coins.

N/S Black - refers to Non-Serialized coins in which the first-bits appear in black text. They are the first coins produced by Lealana. They do not have a serial number on the hologram like newer coins do.

Black - refers to coins which have serial numbers but have the first-bits in black type.

B/F Black - refers to a very small number of coins which have a black first-bit text, but were nevertheless marked as 'BUYER FUNDED'.

Green - refers to coins which were sold after Lealana changed operations after the 'money transmitting' issues that caused Casascius to cease most operations. These coins use green type for the first-bit address.

Image Credits: Lealana

Lealana

1 LTC

Manufacturer: Lealana
Year: 2013
Denomination: 1 LTC
Type: PF, BF, UF

Sub-Type	Mintage
N/S Black	2,000
Black	2,960
B/F Black	40
Green	5,000
Total	**10,000**

Material: Nickel Plated Brass
Diameter: 30 mm
Thickness: 2 mm
Weight: 10 g
Country: USA

This coin was the first released by Lealana, and is the most common due to its very high mintage. Of these coins, the 'first run' (N/S Black) type is generally the most desired by collectors. The 'first run' coins actually have a cleaner appearance on the front, because the 'pitted' coins have a visible circular 'dent' across the 'L', caused by the manufacturing process of creating the 'pit' on the back.

Many Lealana coins including this have a fourth 'sub-type' that is very rare, though its coins technically belong to the 'Black' sub-type. These coins are marked 'BUYER FUNDED' even though their first-bit text is black instead of green as it normally is for such coins. Of all 1 LTC coins, about 40 have this abnormality which will henceforth be referred to as 'Buyer Funded Black'; or B/F Black for short.

Image Credits (clockwise): Elias Ahonen (all)

Lealana

5 LTC Silver

Manufacturer: Lealana
Year: 2013
Denomination: 5 LTC
Type: PF, BF, UF

Sub-Type	Mintage
N/S Black	500
Black	490
B/F Black	10
Green	1,000
Total	**2,000**

Material: .999 Silver
Diameter: 25 mm
Thickness: 1.4 mm
Weight: 0.25 ozt
Country: USA

The silver Lealana coins such as this one are visually cleaner compared to the 1 LTC coins, due to their superior finish and higher quality. It is similar to the Casascius 0.1 BTC coin released in the same year, both having virtually the same quantity of silver. The hologram is nearly identical to the original hologram of the 1 LTC coin, but to a smaller scale with some minor aspects re-arranged.

Image Credits (clockwise): Elias Ahonen (all)

Lealana

10 LTC Silver

Manufacturer: Lealana
Year: 2013
Denomination: 10 LTC
Type: PF, BF, UF

Sub-Type	Mintage
N/S Black	500
Black	490
B/F Black	10
Green	1,000
Total	**2,000**

Material: .999 Silver
Diameter: 30 mm
Thickness: 2 mm
Weight: 0.5 ozt
Country: USA

The first 1,000 of these coins did not include a private key 'pit' on the back side, and thus a small 'bump' can be discerned on the hologram surface because the small round piece of paper containing the private key is placed directly between the flat metal surface and sticker. These are popularly known as 'error coins'. This 'structural stress' has been documented to cause some damage to the hologram even for those that are properly stored, such as in the specimen pictured below (above the 'L' and below the first-bits).

Image Credits (clockwise): Howard Kesselman (2), Took Groth

Lealana

25 LTC Silver

Manufacturer: Lealana
Year: 2013
Denomination: 25 LTC
Type: PF, BF, UF

Sub-Type	Mintage
N/S Black	0
Black	495
B/F Black	0
Green	5
Total	**500**

Material: .999 Silver
Diameter: 39 mm
Thickness: 3 mm
Weight: 1 ozt
Country: USA

This coin can be viewed as a 'litecoin equivalent' of the 25 BTC or 1 BTC Silver Casascius coins (front and back of both pictured below). It is virtually identical in form to the two coins in terms of design, mintage, and denomination. The most striking similarity is the edge along the back side, which is composed of 1's and 0's spelling "Vires in Numeris" in Hawaiian via binary. Another notable aspect of this coin is the 'laser rimming' which followed Casascius' example of adding an extra security feature to premium coins. A small number of these coins have no laser rim. Due to its rarity, this is perhaps the most coveted Lealana coin. The green-address version is the rarest Lealana coin, of which three are marked buyer funded and two are not. The 'binary edge' pattern has since been used in other coins.

Image Credits (clockwise): Howard Kesselman (2)

Lealana

0.1 BTC Brass

Manufacturer: Lealana
Year: 2013
Denomination: 0.1 BTC
Type: PF, BF, UF

Sub-Type	Mintage
N/S Black	0
Black	400
B/F Black	100
Green	9,500
Total	**10,000**

Material: Brass
Diameter: 30 mm
Thickness: 2 mm
Weight: 10 g
Country: USA

Image Credits (clockwise): Elias Ahonen (all)

Like the 25 LTC coin, this is another example of a coin closely inspired by Casascius (which is only natural, as Casascius had been the only major manufacturer from which to draw inspiration). This coin is the perfect example of Lealana walking in the footsteps of Casascius by producing something extremely similar to the 2013 brass 1 BTC coin (the most common Casascius coin) but differentiating. In this case the differentiation was the denomination, which made the coins even more affordable and easy to give away.

It is the cheapest coin in the Lealana Series 2 series, and though its design elements are the same, it is the 'odd one out' as the only non-silver coin in the series.

Lealana

0.1 BTC Silver

Manufacturer: Lealana
Year: 2013
Denomination: 0.1 BTC
Type: PF, BF, UF

Sub-Type	Mintage
N/S Black	0
Black	490
B/F Black	10
Green	1,500
Total	**2,000**

Material: .999 Silver
Diameter: 25 mm
Thickness: 1.4 mm
Weight: 0.25 ozt
Country: USA

Unlike its brass counterpart, the hologram on this coin features a silver 'B' as opposed to gold, giving a more pleasing color match for the all-silver coin.

While the 25 LTC and 0.1 BTC brass coins very closely mimic certain Casascius coins, this coin is actually a direct counterpart to the 0.1 BTC coin made by Casascius. In addition to being released in the same year, it has the exact same weight, metal composition, and denomination. The 0.1 BTC Casascius coin is pictured below.

Image Credits (clockwise): Howard Kesselman (2), Elias Ahonen (2)

Lealana

0.25 BTC Silver

Manufacturer: Lealana
Year: 2013
Denomination: 0.25 BTC
Type: PF, BF, UF

Sub-Type	Mintage
Gold N/S Black	200
Black	290
B/F Black	10
Green	700
Total	**1,200**

Material: .999 Silver
Diameter: 30 mm
Thickness: 2 mm
Weight: 0.5 ozt
Country: USA

This is the first 'quarter bitcoin' and follows the 'Series 2' coin format. Like the 0.1 BTC silver Lealana coin, this coin's hologram features a silver 'B'. Notably, over 25 specimens are known to actually have the 'Gold B' (pictured) hologram normally reserved for the 0.1 BTC Brass and 1 BTC Lealana coins. It is possible that one or more 'B/F Black' coins were also subject to this abnormality, making them extremely rare.

Pictured in this entry is a unique custom Lealana coin set owned by Scott Barnett who had it made specially to honor his son. It contains 3 coins, all with gold holograms and a unique blue public address font. All coins are funded, with the addresses: 1Dexter (1 BTC), 1Woody (0.5 BTC), and 1Barnett (0.25 BTC).

Image Credits (clockwise): Howard Kesselman (2), Dexter Barnett (1)

Lealana

0.5 BTC Silver

Manufacturer: Lealana
Year: 2013
Denomination: 0.5 BTC
Type: PF, BF, UF

Sub-Type	Mintage
Gold N/S Black	200
Black	290
B/F Black	10
Green	200
Total	**700**

Material: .999 Silver
Diameter: 39 mm
Thickness: 3 mm
Weight: 1 ozt
Country: USA

While the front has no variance from the other coins in the series, the back presents something new. Instead of a full 'binary edge' as one might guess from first glance, it actually features a 'partial binary edge' (the first of its kind) around the hologram, while the rest of the coin is made up of a sparkling 'bumpy' minted surface.

Like the 0.1 BTC and 0.25 BTC silver Lealana coins, this coin's hologram features a silver 'B'. Notably, at least 10 specimens are known to actually have the 'Gold B' hologram normally reserved for the 0.1 BTC Brass and 1 BTC Lealana coins. It is possible that one or more 'B/F Black' coins were also subject to this abnormality, making them extremely rare.

Image Credits (clockwise): Howard Kesselman (all)

Lealana

1 BTC Silver 'Gold B'

Manufacturer: Lealana
Year: 2013
Denomination: 1 BTC
Type: PF, BF, UF

Sub-Type	Mintage
N/S Black	0
Black	290
B/F Black	10
Green	200
Total	**500**

Material: .999 Silver
Diameter: 39 mm
Thickness: 3 mm
Weight: 1 ozt
Country: USA

This is the only Lealana coin with gold plating, and is perhaps the most visually interesting due to the stark contrast which highlights the 'B' and hologram. It is the same size and weight as the 0.5 BTC coin of the same series, but the 'partial binary edge' is replaced by a flat, smooth gold plated surface on which the hologram is placed. The hologram for this coin is the same as for the 0.1 BTC brass coin; featuring a gold 'B' instead of a silver one.

The coin can be seen as a direct counterpart and competitor to the Casascius 1 BTC 'Gold B' Series 3 2013 coin, as both were released in the same year with identical specs. Compare to it below.

Image Credits (clockwise): Howard Kesselman (2)

Lealana

Hybrid Coins

Manufacturer: Lealana
Year Released: 2015
Denomination: 1 BTC, 5 BTC
Type: BF

Sub-Type	Mintage
1 BTC	1
5 BTC	1
Total	**2**

Material:
Nickel Pl. Brass (5 BTC)
Brass (1 BTC)
Diameter: 28.5 mm
Thickness: 1.7 mm
Weight: 7.4 g
Country: USA

These coins consist of redeemed Casascius coins with Lealana holograms affixed. These were auctioned by Lealana and buyers were required to fund them prior to dispatch. Lealana has declared the coins to be unique; no additional hybrids will be made with the same type of Casascius coins. The existence of these coins could be taken to demonstrate the respect Lealana places on Casascius coins, as well as a recognition that collectors of Lealana coins consider both brands to be central to the formation of physical crypto-currency.

Image Credits (clockwise): Lealana (all)

LuckyBit

Silver Plated Wallet

Manufacturer: LuckyBit
Year: 2016
Denomination: BTC
Type: PF, DIY

Material	Mintage
Silver Pl. Zinc Alloy	100
.999 Silver	10
Zinc Alloy	6
Total	**116**

Diameter: 39 mm
Thickness: 3 mm
Weight: 35 g (Alloy), 1 ozt (.999)
Country: Curacao

LuckyBit is a Bitcoin gambling website. It works by allowing users to send BTC to certain addresses which then return it in various multiples such as x0.2, x1.2, x3, x99, etcetera according to calculated chance. At the time of writing, nearly 100,000 BTC has been wagered on the site. LuckyBit created these coins as promotional items to advertise the website. Though the majority of coins are silver plated, ten .999 Silver coins were created exclusively for employees of the site. In addition six non-plated rounds were produced as a test strike, one of which was auctioned off.

The front of the coin declares LuckyBit as the '#1 Bitcoin Game', and features an image of the game as it appears on the website ('bitcoins' drop down into slots in real-time corresponding to the multiplier). Gears are a central theme on both the back and front, with the pattern on the back's outer rim resembling a gear. These gears refer directly to the game theme, but more indirectly symbolize the precise engineering behind crypto-currency. The coin has a small hologram compared to its size, and the back has repeating text of the LuckyBit website and 'LuckyBit' to encourage viewers of the coin to visit the site. Each coin is serialized.

Image Credits (clockwise): Howard Kesselman (all)

Microsoul

In June 2013, Matthew Rodbourne of the UK began selling a 1 BTC physical Bitcoin, and six months later released a new batch as he branded his business 'Microsoul'. Finding demand, he went on to release a total of six different coins, and remains active. His coins have clearly been heavily inspired by Casascius' classic designs, to such an extent that a casual observer taking a quick glance at both might not realize that two independent producers are involved. With coins in 0.01 BTC and 0.05 BTC, Microsoul very much worked on the same scale of value as Casascius did originally, with the 0.01 BTC and 0.05 BTC coins very closely resembling the equivalent dollar values of the 1 BTC and 5 BTC Casascius coins only two years earlier. With the motto of 'Microsoul coins for the masses', the stated purpose of the venture has been to deliver reliable, cost effective, and interesting physical Bitcoins to all who might want them.

Microsoul does not aim to make a substantial profit, and is very much a personal hobby rather than a for-profit enterprise. He has collaborated with Crypto Imperator, another producer to assist in making the 1,000,000 DOGE Gold Coin a reality.

Matthew has been very active in the crypto-currency community outside of producing physical coins. In 2014 he participated in the release a free mobile game called 'The Ponz' in which a superhero named 'Ponz' must avoid hitting aircraft and central banks as he flies forward while collecting bitcoins and World Aid Coins in the sky. These 'World Aid Coins' tie in with another project headed by Rodbourne: the creation of a new crypto currency in which 50 percent of the currency which is 'mined' goes into a fund to be put towards various humanitarian causes. The currency would function by having a few dozen designated 'guardians' from various backgrounds who vote upon the causes that should be supported. The aim is that if 'WAC' gains a large user-base, its use would have a humanitarian benefit on the world at large. A designated Internet forum was created for the concept, and Microsoul designed special 'guardian' silver coins to be given to the 'trustees' of the currency. As of printing, World Aid Coin does not appear to have any active user base or market value.

Image Credits: Microsoul

'Zombie error' coins and other setbacks

In 2014, Matthew discovered an error in the program that was used to create the bitcoin addresses of the coins, causing some faulty 'zombie' 0.01 BTC coins that did not actually contain any redeemable BTC being sold to unsuspecting buyers. Though the coins had technically been 'funded', the font of the private keys was incorrect and caused some characters to be missing, making them un-redeemable. Matthew's quality control procedure of peeling and redeeming every 100th coin proved useful in this situation, as otherwise thousands of coins could have been spoiled and tens of bitcoins lost.

As soon as the error was discovered, buyers were contacted and a quiet recall took place. The vast majority of coins were successfully returned to Microsoul for replacement, but around 20 are still believed to be in private ownership. Had this critical issue been discovered by a buyer instead of Microsoul, a very significant backlash from the Bitcoin community may have taken place, and serious reputation damage to the entire physical Bitcoin market may have followed. The incident is an important reminder of an important caveat regarding most physical Bitcoins; the owner of a coin must have faith in the producer. The truth is that with coins functioning as simple 'bitcoin wallets', it is virtually impossible to verify that the producer did not keep a copy of the private keys to each coin, be the copy in a digital, printed, or photographic format. To downplay these fears, the majority of manufacturers selling physical bitcoins have been purposeful in making their identities public knowledge, in a sector that generally puts a high value on anonymity. Matthew himself actually displayed a scanned copy of his passport on his website, to convince buyers that he had no intention of keeping private keys of his coins.

Another major setback happened during the production of silver coins in China. Upon receiving the initial batch of coins, he was unsatisfied and sent back 90 percent of them to be fixed. Receiving the improved coins sometime later, he was still unhappy with the quality of work. Upon sending them back to the manufacturer a second time, the coins were confiscated by Chinese customs, causing Microsoul a loss of about 10,000 USD.

Below: 'The Ponz' featuring the World Aid Coin logo, and a sample design for the silver 'Guardian Coins' to be distributed to the 'trustees' of the new currency.

Image Credits (clockwise): Microsoul (all)

Microsoul

PBC Coin

Manufacturer: Microsoul
Year: 2013
Denomination: 1 BTC
Type: PF, UF

Version	Mintage
Funded (PF)	62
Blanks (UF)	38
TOTAL	**100**

Mat.: Gold Pl. Brass & Nickel
Diameter: 40 mm
Thickness: 3 mm
Weight: 31 g
Country: UK

The first coin produced by Matthew, the 1BTC 2013 coin was created before the 'Microsoul' brand, and is thus quite different from his later designs. The coin itself is extremely generic and simple, inscribed only with '1 Bitcoin' in raised gold letters.

Of the 100 minted, 62 were funded and the remainder were sold as blanks. 50 coins remain funded. This coin is unique in its operation. While most similar coins simply include a private key like a paper wallet, the private key on this coin is not actually the private key per se, but a written code representing it. Buyers of this coin received a piece of paper containing a simple equation to decrypt the code. A list of coins is maintained by the Microsoul website, with the name/screen-name of each owner publicly visible. In the event that a coin is transferred or sold, the seller should include the original private code received with the coin, or else the concealed BTC cannot be redeemed without assistance from Microsoul who maintains a copy of each decryption code. A further point of interest with this coin is that the private key code is actually engraved to the back of the coin, instead of on a piece of paper behind the sticker.

Image Credits (clockwise): Howard Kesselman, Microsoul

Microsoul

0.01 BTC

Manufacturer: Microsoul
Year: 2013, 2014
Denomination: 0.01 BTC
Type: PF

Version	Mintage
2013 Series 1	407
2014 Series 1	124
2014 Series 2	50
TOTAL	**581**

Material: Brass
Diameter: 28.5 mm
Thickness: 1.1 mm
Weight: 6.2 g
Country: UK

The first Microsoul branded coin, it displays a nearly identical face to the classic Casascius brass coin. The brand is however easily distinguished by the devil head logo to the left of the Bitcoin symbol on the front face. Being the first coin bearing the logo, it received a mixed reception with some expressing that it was distracting and irrelevant.

The 2014 version of this coin is the one affected by the Zombie error.

Some of Microsoul's Series 2 hologram was placed on a very small number of 2014 coins, creating a very rare sub-type (2014 Series 2).

Image Credits (clockwise): Elias Ahonen, Howard Kesselman, Elias Ahonen

Microsoul

2014 0.01 BTC Silver Coin

Manufacturer: Microsoul
Year: 2014
Denomination: 0.01 BTC
Type: PF

Version	Mintage
2014 Series 1	5
2014 Series 2	41
TOTAL	**46**

Material: Silver (>90%)
Diameter: 28.5 mm
Thickness: 1.1 mm
Weight: 15 g
Country: UK

These coins were manufactured in China, and caused a large amount of trouble for Microsoul. The photo on the right ('2014 Series 2*' in the chart) is what Microsoul originally received 400 of from the Chinese manufacturer, but being unsatisfied with quality, sent back to be re-done. Microsoul was still unsatisfied, and shipped 90 percent of the coins back for a second time. Unfortunately, these coins were lost to customs resulting in a loss of over 10,000 USD. It is theoretically possible that an additional 359 unfunded coins without holograms will surface one day.

Microsoul was hesitant about releasing these coins at all, as the quality was questionable. However, he made the best of his losses and sold these coins for 40 USD each. He has confirmed them to be at least 90 percent silver via acid tests (a common way to determine gold or silver content using an chemical solution).

Each coin is funded and sealed with the Microsoul Series 2 hologram. Only five coins with the Series 1 hologram (photo on the left) were made as gifts to re-sellers and are very rare.

Image Credits (clockwise): Howard Kesselman, Microsoul

Microsoul

0.05 BTC 1/2 Troy Oz. Silver Coin

Manufacturer: Microsoul
Year: 2014, 2016
Denomination: 0.05 BTC
Type: PF

Version	Mintage
2014 Gold B Series 1	140
2014 Silver Series 2	28
2016 Silver Series 3	40
2016 Gold B Series 3	40
2016 Silver Series 3 (Red Font)	10
2016 Gold B Series 3 (Red Font)	10
TOTAL	**268***

Material: .999 Silver
Diameter: 28.5 mm
Thickness: 2.25 mm
Weight: 0.5 ozt
Country: UK

This coin was the first of Microsoul's silver releases. While the majority have a golden rim, logo, and 'B', 152 are pure silver. Of the all-silver coins, 28 have been fitted with Microsoul's Series 2 hologram sticker (Pictured). Each coin is engraved with '____ of 1000' on the side.

*All numbers are approximate

Image Credits (clockwise): Elias Ahonen, Howard Kesselman (2)

Microsoul

Lucky Coin

Manufacturer: Microsoul
Year: 2016*
Denomination: 0.01 BTC**
Type: PF

Version	Mintage
Round 1	10
Round 2	10
Round 3	10
Round 4	10
Round 5	10
TOTAL* **	**50**

Material: Brass
Diameter: 28.5 mm
Thickness: 1.1 mm
Weight: 6.2 g
Country: UK
*Both 2013 and 2014 coins used
**10% have 1.01 BTC balance
***At time of writing

The Lucky Coin is a very unique and innovative product created by Microsoul using the series three hologram. These coins have a private key, but their public key is not visible. In its place, '#[round number].[coin number] LUCKY' is seen through the window on the custom hologram. The 'game' works as follows: every week, ten buyers purchase a Lucky Coin for 0.15 BTC each. Every coin is funded with 0.01 BTC, but a random one is funded with an additional 1 BTC bringing the total to 1.01 BTC for one of the ten coins. In essence, this coin is a lottery ticket with a twist. What makes this much more than a scratch-and-win card is the unique community aspect. The ten public keys are released publicly, so that everyone knows how many coins in a set have been peeled and if the 1.01 BTC coin is still un-peeled. Often, buyers will announce whether they plan on peeling or not. As more coins in a set are peeled without the prize being found, the value of remaining coins will increase as their probability of containing the prize is higher. This game has drawn lots of collector involvement, encouraging commentary and speculation amongst participants.

Image Credits (clockwise): Elias Ahonen, Howard Kesselman

Mike Murphy

MaxCoin Silver Cryptobullion 2014

Manuf.	Mike Murphy
Year	2014
Denom.	100 MAX
Type	UF
Mintage	5,000
Material	.999 Silver
Diameter	39 mm
Thickness	3 mm
Weight	1 ozt
Country	Ireland

These silver coins are designed to hold Maxcoin, which is an alternative crypto-currency launched by Max Keiser, a broadcaster who hosts *The Keiser Report*, a financial commentary show on *Russia Today UK*. The coins are created by an individual named Mike Murphy, who started a successful online crowd-funder that raised 89,108 USD. The amount raised is a huge one, and is largely a result of the publicity afforded by Mr. Keiser's involvement with Maxcoin. Keiser is known for his statements in favor of silver over many other investments, which makes it appropriate that the minted Maxcoin is of a silver composition.

The front features the Maxcoin 'm' logo, surrounded by a circuit board similar to the design which was first used by MJB Monetary Metals. In addition to 'maxcoin' the year is displayed along with the Latin phrase 'Defendit Numerus' which translates to 'There is safety in numbers'.

Image Credits (clockwise): Howard Kesselman (all)

MJB Monetary Metals

MJB Monetary Metals was a small venture undertaken by Mike Bruce of the United Kingdom. In addition to three Bitcoin rounds, MJB Monetary Metals has created some other unrelated copper rounds. The great significance of MJB monetary metals is the fact that it was the very first producer of coins with any kind of Bitcoin theme. Though the 1 gram silver coins were cheap, they were obviously well over the silver spot price. One reason it is much higher was the 20% VAT (tax) imposed on silver in the UK, which discouraged some prospective buyers.

The third and final coin produced is copper and features an iconic 'circuit board' design, and was produced by The Mulligan Mint with a share of profits going to Mr. Bruce. The Mulligan Mint eventually failed and faced numerous legal issues. The coin has become one of the most popular representations of Bitcoin, with its images being featured in hundreds of news articles. Though the coin was pure copper, Chinese manufacturers have begun selling gold, silver, and copper clad copies at wholesale prices without the authorization of Mr. Bruce.

Image Credits (clockwise): MJB Monetary Metals (all)

MJB Monetary Metals

Series 1 Silver

Manuf.	MJB Monetary Metals
Year	2011
Denom.	BTC
Type	Round
Mintage	1,000
Material	.999 Silver
Diameter	15 mm
Thickness	0.75 mm
Weight	1 g
Country	USA

This is the first bitcoin themed coin to be produced and sold. Released on June 28th, 2011, these were sold out over a month before the first Casascius coins went on sale. Being sold for £1.50 each with a minimum order of 10, supply ran out in two months. Due to the initial cheapness of these coins, it is likely that many were damaged by mishandling and/or misplaced over the years. As such, the number of these coins in good condition is likely very small, and one coming onto the market is a rare event.

Image Credits (clockwise): Andrew Dobbins (all)

MJB Monetary Metals

Series 2 Silver

Manuf.	MJB Monetary Metals
Year	2011
Denom.	BTC
Type	Round
Mintage	1,000
Material	.999 Silver
Diameter	15 mm
Thickness	0.75 mm
Weight	1 g
Country	USA

After the success of the v1 "Type 1" silver rounds, a second version was released in August, about a week before the Casascius coins came into existence. This coin is an aesthetic improvement to the first coin, in that the 'B' is clear easily visible. Like its counterpart, it features a 'binary theme' of 1's and 0's, with the back side having an outer rim is 1's and 0's. This rim inspired the 'binary ring' feature in many physical Bitcoins, including Casascius, Lealana, and Cryptolator. It appears shinier when compared to the v1 coin. On the upper right, a one has been converted to jewelry.

Image Credits (clockwise): Andrew Dobbins (2), Unknown (1)

MJB Monetary Metals

Series 1 Copper

Manuf.	MJB Monetary Metals
Year	2012
Denom.	BTC
Type	Round
Mintage	
Material	.999 Copper
Diameter	39 mm
Thickness	3 mm
Weight	1 ozt
Country	USA

This coin was designed by Mike Bruce, and produced and distributed by a third party mint on a profit-sharing agreement. The round has a circuit board theme, emphasizing the technological aspect of Bitcoin. The design originated from an artistic drawing, and is referred to as an 'Art Round' by Mr. Bruce. The coin and its design has become an extremely popular 'image' for Bitcoin and is used as the primary photo in countless news articles and even some books related to Bitcoin. These coins have been the subject of copying by Chinese manufacturers and subsequent wholesale. These (authentic) coins are pure copper, whereas the Chinese copies are silver, gold, or copper clad iron coins.

Image Credits (clockwise): Unknown (all)

Nasty Mining

Nasty Mining is not a traditional physical crypto-coin producer (if the word 'traditional' could ever be used for the subject), but rather a 'Bitcoin mining operation' run by an anonymous individual known as 'OgNasty'.

NastyFans is a sort of 'club' with 30,000 'seats' (memberships). It's premise is unusual: it is an 'unofficial fan club' of 'Nasty Mining' which is run by another anonymous individual known as 'nonnakip'. 'Seats' can be bought from the club, or they can be bought and sold like an asset amongst members. 'Nasty Mining' donates all of the bitcoins it mines to the club along with half of revenue from coin sales. In turn, 75% of these donations are distributed amongst the 30,000 'Seats' while the remaining 25% is saved for mining equipment purchases. Thus, owners of 'Seats' regularly get BTC deposits. This makes the seats somewhat comparable to shares in a bitcoin mining co-operative, though this system is much more unique.

The club has created its own mining pool 'NastyPool', iOS app, Windows app, shirts, and two types of coins. The first type of coins are simply promotional keepsakes, whereas the second type are much more special. The second type are known as 'Minted Seats'. These come in 1, 2, and 5 seat denominations. The receiving address of bitcoin 'donations' for the seat(s) is the same as the coin's, and these proceeds are thus secured by the hologram. They are the only coins that receive planned BTC deposits, though they are not guaranteed. Each coin's public key begins with a version of a sequential '1Nasty' address unique to the coin's version. The coins themselves are produced and sold by OgNasty.

What exactly is a 'mining pool'? It is a significant network of computers which pool processing power to mine bitcoins as one entity. As large numbers of computers are constantly running calculations to 'uncover' bitcoin, an essentially random computer is awarded a 'block' of bitcoin at every given interval. This means that a normal computer mining bitcoins alone is an incredibly risky undertaking, because the likelihood of finding a 'block' is so unpredictable and could easily take several years. The solution is to connect the bitcoin miner to a mining pool which has a statistically larger chance of mining a predictable amount of bitcoin. Individual owners of computers are then paid for their share of the pool's processing power (for example, a pool earning 10 BTC per day would pay 0.1 BTC to a computer contributing 1% of the computing power.

Image Credits: Nasty Mining

Nasty Mining

1oz .999 Silver Minted Seat

Manuf.	Nasty Mining
Year	2014
Denom.	1 'Seat'
Type	PF
Mintage	500
Material	.999 Silver
Diameter	39 mm
Thickness	3 mm
Weight	1 ozt
Country	USA

This coin is the first of its kind in many ways. Though it does not specify a bitcoin balance, it will likely receive allotments of BTC well into the future. As explained in the Mint Bio, this coin functions not unlike an ownership share to a company into which small dividends are paid and a fundraiser with 50% of the coin's sale price being donated to NastyFans. It's BTC value is therefore ever-increasing, assuming that the pay-outs do not stop. The public key address of the coin is engraved along the rim of the coin. The face of the coin lacks many features that 'physical bitcoins' generally possess, such as bitcoin symbols and other imagery alluding to bitcoin (though it does include two images of bitcoin miners). It is simply a logo, which is out of place when compared to other silver bitcoins.

Image Credits (clockwise): Howard Kesselman (all)

Nasty Mining

5oz .999 Silver Minted Seats

Manuf.	Nasty Mining
Year	2015
Denom.	5 'Seats'
Type	PF
Mintage	100
Material	.999 Silver
Diameter	2.5 in
Thickness	6 mm
Weight	5 ozt
Country	USA

This coin is the largest and heaviest physical crypto-coin produced to date, weighing in at 5 oz of pure silver with a proof-like finish. It's public key is engraved above the hologram (engraving process and a close-up are pictured on the right), which serves as the deposit address of five Seats as explained in the Mint Bio. Its face is nearly identical to the 1 Seat coin, though its Seat number and weight markings differ. The back has the 'Nasty' hologram, along with the logos of 'Nasty Mining', 'Nasty Fans' and 'Nasty Pool'. Due to its size, it has been referred to as a 'hockey puck' by some prospective buyers.

Image Credits (clockwise): Howard Kesselman, bitcointalk.org user 'OgNasty' (2), Howard Kesselman

Nasty Mining

Hybrid Casascius 2012 5 BTC

Manuf.	Nasty Mining
Year	2014
Denom.	5 BTC
Type	UF
Mintage	20
Material	Nickel Pl. Brass
Diameter	28.5 mm
Thickness	1.7 mm
Weight	7.4 g
Country	USA

This coin is made from an empty Casascius 5 BTC coin, with a 'Nasty Mining' hologram added to the back. The public key is printed onto the hologram, and the coin is shipped unfunded. 20 were made and sold for 0.25 BTC each via the Bitcointalk.org forum. The slab it comes with has a QR code pertaining to the public key, allowing for easy funding by the buyer.

Image Credits (clockwise): bitcointalk.org user 'OgNasty' (all)

Nasty Mining

1g .999 Silver Collector Round

Manuf.	Nasty Mining
Year	2013
Denom.	BTC
Type	Round
Mintage	1,000
Material	.999 Silver
Diameter	15 mm
Thickness	0.75 mm
Weight	1 g
Country	USA

The first coin produced by Nasty Mining, the coin immortalizes the '1NastyF' vanitygen address used by NastyFans as it's donation address. It also features a central image of a Bitcoin miner hardware piece. These coins were directly inspired by the `MJB Monetary Metals` 1 gram silver rounds which were released a few months earlier. The reverse rim spells out '2013' in binary code, which is an idea originally implemented by Casascius and later adopted by many manufacturers including Lealana and Cryptolator, among others. There is no numeric year stamp, which is quite unique.

Image Credits (clockwise): bitcointalk.org user 'OgNasty' (all)

Nasty Mining

1g .999 Silver NastyPool Collector Round

Manuf.	Nasty Mining
Year	2014
Denom.	BTC
Type	Round
Mintage	1,000
Material	.999 Silver
Diameter	15 mm
Thickness	0.75 mm
Weight	1 g
Country	USA

Following the design of the previous year's coin, this coin features a prominent 'Nasty Pool' logo and '2014' in Binary code on the back rim along with the '1NastyP' 'vanity address' used by NastyPool. A 'Vanity address' is a specially generated crypto-currency wallet in which the 'first-bits' are not random but intentional, in the same way as someone might order 'vanity plates' for a car.

Image Credits (clockwise): Elias Ahonen (all)

New Liberty

2013 Silver Bitcoin Specie

Manufacturer: New Liberty
Year: 2013
Denomination: 0.25 BTC
Type: Round

Version	Mintage
Silver	2,900
Gold Pl Silver	100
TOTAL	**3,000**

Material: .999 Silver
Diameter: 39 mm
Thickness: 3 mm
Weight: 1 ozt
Country: USA

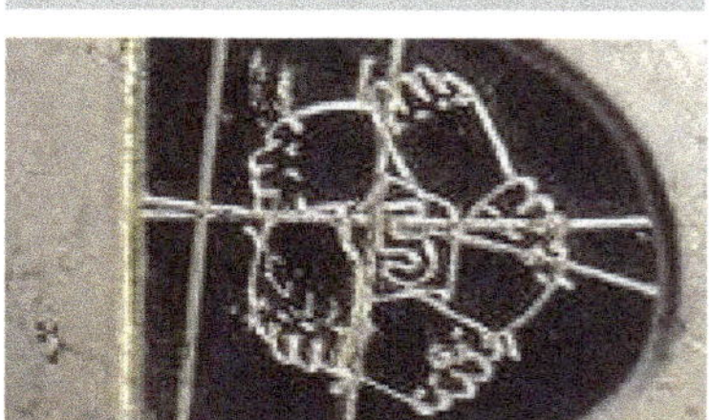

The word 'specie' refers to money in non-paper form, which might refer to the silver content of the coin, the coin itself (as opposed to paper money), to the Bitcoin theme, or all three. The rounds have a 'denomination' of 0.25 BTC, which at the time of production was very close to the spot price of 1 troy ounce of silver. The QR code on the back opens a webpage that displays the current price of an ounce of silver in BTC. Several counterfeits of the coin have been made in China.

While the majority of these rounds are pure silver, 100 (serialized) rounds are gold electro-plated. There are two additional varieties of this coin, differentiated by 'hallmarks' on the coins themselves. The first of these is the 'Satoshi White Paper fifth Anniversary' hallmark composed of five hands surrounding the number '5' which can be found inside of the Bitcoin 'B' on 100 coins (pictured on the lower left). The other variety is called the 'Pizza Day Commemorative' hallmark, composed of two round pizzas with '10K BTC' engraved under them in reference to the first bitcoin transaction where two pizzas were bought for 10,000 BTC. It is found above the '0.25 BTC' mark.

Image Credits (clockwise): Howard Kesselman (2), bitcointalk.org user 'bitcoininformation'

New Liberty

2014 Silver Bitcoin Specie

Manuf.	New Liberty
Year	2014
Denom.	.01 BTC
Type	Round
Mintage	
Material	.999 Silver
Diameter	39 mm
Thickness	3 mm
Weight	1 ozt
Country	USA

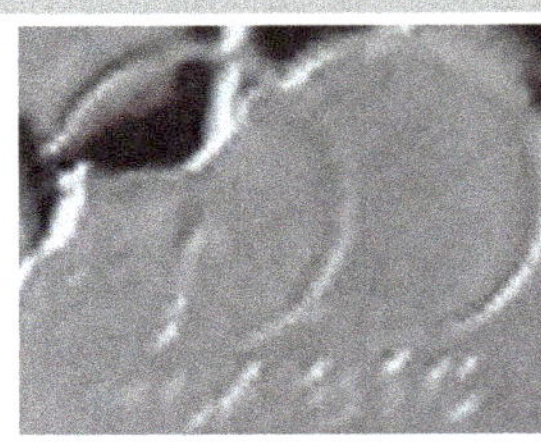

Released after the 0.25 BTC denominated round, this round is identical except its denomination is only 10mBTC (0.01 BTC) and the year is 2014.

An image of the 'Pizza Day Commemorative' hallmark is shown on the right (hallmarks are found on 2013 coins only).

Image Credits (clockwise): Howard Kesselman, New Liberty, Howard Kesselman

NOLACOIN

The New Orleans Bitcoin Exchange LLC was incorporated in 2011 by founder Arash Dini, who is an orthopedic surgeon. Though Mr. Dini lived in Florida at the time, his company was incorporated in Louisiana due to the regulatory laws regarding 'investment banking' being more permissive. One might wonder what physical Bitcoins might have to do with investment banking (especially since it was 2011, when the very first physical bitcoins were being created), but it must be understood that the company's business plans were much more complex than the minting of rounds or loading crypto-currency into coins.

The idea was to create what is essentially a Bitcoin bank, issuing physical coins that are guaranteed to be redeemable for the face-value of BTC. This would have meant that those using the exchange would not be holding any 'real' BTC, but instead an 'I Owe You' from the company in much the similar way as US currency was representative and redeemable for gold bullion during the time of the Gold Standard in the USA. The idea of was to allow anyone to own bitcoin in a material way that they could understand. This business never materialized due to the amount of regulation and other complications that such a venture would encounter, not least of which was the fact that credit card companies refused to allow their cards to be used for New Orleans Bitcoin Exchange purchases. Despite the initial failure, it should be noted that Arash Dini was one of the first individuals (along with Casascius' Mike Caldwell) to give Bitcoin a physical form that could be transferable between individuals in a physical manner.

Though it is true that the framework would have required complete trust in the New Orleans Bitcoin Exchange's ability and willingness to secure its stored BTC and allow it to be redeemed for coins, it should not be forgotten that essentially all physical crypto-currency manufacturers demand a similar level of confidence because there is theoretically little to stop them from secretly recording all private keys and emptying 'secure' coins at will. When considering this overall plan, it is clear that it went against the 'spirit of Bitcoin', which is meant to be a trust-less currency which is directly held by the owner instead of by a bank or other third party; a fact Mr. Dini himself has admitted. The first series of 'NOLACOIN' coins were originally created for this venture, and though they were intended to be 'coins', they were eventually sold as 'rounds' alongside the newer NOLACOIN coins.

After the initial failure, the business was renamed to NOLACOIN LLC and a series of "traditional physical Bitcoins" was released in June 2014. These make up the true offerings of NOLACOIN.
Image Credits: NOLACOIN

NOLACOIN

1 Bitcoin Token

Manuf.	NOLACOIN
Year	2012
Denom.	1 BTC
Type	Round
Mintage	200
Material	Nickel Pl. Zinc
Diameter	26 mm
Thickness	2.15 mm
Weight	8 g
Country	USA

Though this is listed as a 'round', it was originally intended as a 'coin'. As per the original business plan of New Orleans Bitcoin Exchange (now called NOLACOIN), these coins were meant to function as physical tokens representing real BTC held by the company as if it was a bank. These coins were eventually sold off as rounds as the business venture did not take off as planned, and are undoubtedly an important part of the history of physical crypto-currency. The eight character code engraved on each round serves no practical purpose now, as it was meant to be used in tracking of the BTC-backed coins.

Image Credits (clockwise): Howard Kesselman (all)

NOLACOIN

5 Bitcoin Token

Manuf.	NOLACOIN
Year	2012
Denom.	5 BTC
Type	Round
Mintage	200
Material	Zinc and Gold Pl. Brass
Diameter	31 mm
Thickness	2.15 mm
Weight	12 g
Country	USA

A notable variation in the coins in this series is the artwork surrounding the logo on the backside. It starts off as a simple circle pattern for the 1 BTC round, but upgrades to a more prestigious wreath on the 5 BTC round. The 10 BTC round in turn has a much more substantial and decorative wreath, implying a higher importance. The 5 BTC coin is notable for its two-tone plating. It was created in the same year as the Casascius 5 BTC coin.

10 Bitcoin Token

Manuf.	NOLACOIN
Year	2012
Denom.	10 BTC
Type	Round
Mintage	200
Material	Gold Pl. Brass
Diameter	39 mm
Thickness	2.15 mm
Weight	16 g
Country	USA

Though the rounds in this series vary in color, they have a common design. The outer rim of the front is surrounded by 'B' symbols, while the inner section contains the written denomination and year around the center where the (originally intended) face value of the coin is stated. The outer rim of the backside states 'BITCOIN EXCHANGE OF NEW ORLEANS', with the defunct exchange's logo in the middle.

Image Credits (clockwise): Howard Kesselman (all)

NOLACOIN

Half Bitcoin

Manuf.	NOLACOIN
Year	2014
Denom.	0.5 BTC
Type	PF, UF
Mintage	999
Material	Copper Pl. Brass
Diameter	43 mm
Thickness	2 mm
Weight	23.3 g
Country	USA

The coins in this series have several unique aspects. Instead of having a hologram sticker that is peeled off to access the private key, the holograms on these coins are 'scratch off' surfaces. Upon being scratched (by perhaps, another coin), a QR code and written version of the private key is revealed. Due to the surface being prone to scratch when in contact with any hard object, these coins should be kept in a proper air-tight holder.

An interesting fact about the '1/2 BTC' coin is that its value is marked as a fraction instead of a decimal like all other coins of that denomination.

Image Credits (clockwise): Elias Ahonen (all)

NOLACOIN

One Bitcoin

Manuf.	NOLACOIN
Year	2014
Denom.	1 BTC
Type	PF, UF
Mintage	999
Material	Nickel Pl. Brass
Diameter	43 mm
Thickness	2 mm
Weight	21 g
Country	USA

It is clear that the design concepts in this series reflect those of the first. The backside has virtually the same design, with the logo in the middle and 'BITCOIN EXCHANGE OF NEW ORLEANS' written on the outer rim. On the front, the public key is engraved along with the serial number, surrounded by denomination markings on the outer rim. An interesting thing to note is that each coin in this series is of a slightly different weight.

Three Bitcoin

Manuf.	NOLACOIN
Year	2014
Denom.	3 BTC
Type	PF, UF
Mintage	500
Material	Nickel and Gold Pl. Brass
Diameter	43 mm
Thickness	2 mm
Weight	27.8 g
Country	USA

In addition to the scratch-off hologram (pictured above in action), these coins contain another unique security feature. Each has a gold-tone security sticker around the hologram, which serves several purposes from preventing the removal and replacement of the hologram to preventing the coin from being accidentally scratched in the process of scratching off the hologram. It of course also serves as a visual feature, bearing images of the logo. This is the only physical Bitcoin made in the denomination of three.

Image Credits (clockwise): Howard Kesselman (3), NOLACOIN (1)

Osborne Mint

Bullion Not Bits

Manuf.	Osborne Mint
Year	
Denom.	BTC
Type	Round
Mintage	
Material	.999 Copper
Diameter	
Thickness	
Weight	1 oz
Country	USA

The Osborne Mint markets itself as the oldest private mint in America with roots back to 1835, making it by far the oldest mint to produce anything with a crypto-currency theme. This round is part of a series called 'Safety in Numbers', with other rounds in the series bearing statements such as 'Guns and Gold' and 'Food and Shelter' in a 'survivalist' theme. The statement 'Bullion not Bits' suggests that bullion provides this 'safety' while Bitcoin does not. The image on the front supports this sentiment; the Bitcoin symbol is shown to have less 'weight' on a scale compared to a precious metal coin (which happens to be a 'Walking Liberty' coin) issued by the U.S. Mint. The backside is the same as for other coins in the series, and the statement 'Real Metal, Real Value' is prominent. The mint offers an explanation for its negative views toward Bitcoin, which while not unique, are rather misinformed.

"Baby, when the lights go out, the Internet goes out, and what does that mean? Bitcoins vanish like they never even existed. Who knows how secure Bitcoins really are? They're created by anonymous masterminds. Is there a back-door in the software? Do their Minions have a plan to empty the coffers? Is there a virus to delete all the ownership records? Bullion in a secure and accessible location is a whole lot more useful than a bunch of bits and bytes."[1]

Image Credits (clockwise): Elias Ahonen, John Sacco

1. "BULLION NOT BITS .999 COPPER 1 OZ ROUND" Link: http://osbornemint.com/Bullion_not_Bits_copper_bullion_1_oz_round-1-1-1-1-1.aspx

Ravenbit

Ravenbit has made coins with two designs, the second of which has produced a very notable variety of bronze, antique bronze, copper, and .999 silver. In addition to all these variations, Ravenbit has introduced a complex system of 'colors' to further differentiate coins. Perhaps the most unique Ravenbit coins are the 'planet' coins which are essentially damaged coins that have been given a 'story' and then sold for higher than normal prices.

All Ravenbit coins come with a branded felt pouch and display stand. The presentation and packaging of Ravenbit is perhaps the most professional of all similar manufacturers. A significant number of Ravenbit coins have been graded by ANACS, with the best coins receiving grades of MS-67 and MS-68. Uniquely among manufacturers, Ravenbit actually sells graded coins directly to customers, removing the need for them to spend their time, effort, and money to get the coins graded.

Below: The contents of a normal coin order (left), and a hologram being peeled (right)

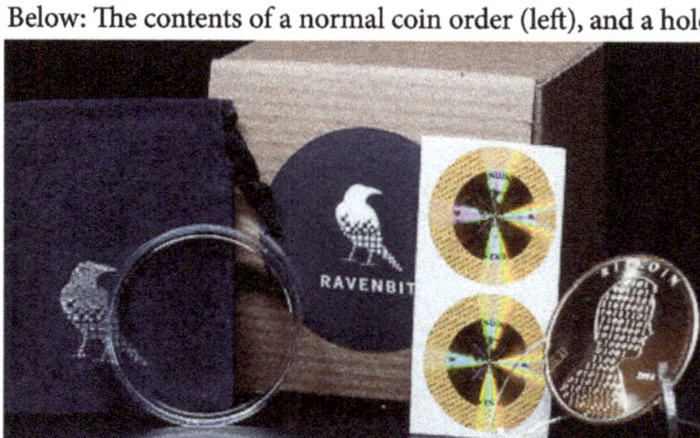

Image Credits (clockwise): Ravenbit (all)

Ravenbit

Series 1.0 - Satoshi

Manuf.	Ravenbit
Year	2013
Denom.	BTC
Type	DIY
Mintage	Brass
Material	204
Diameter	39 mm
Thickness	3 mm
Weight	26.9 g
Country	USA

This round is a tribute to Satoshi Nakamoto, the anonymous individual (or group) responsible for the Bitcoin code. The face of the round has the outline of a person, with no facial features signifying anonymity. The anonymous person is filled with 1's and 0's, which spell out 'Satoshi Nakamoto' in binary. Unlike later Ravenbit coins and rounds, these do not have a private key pit.

Image Credits (clockwise): Elias Ahonen, Ravenbit

Ravenbit

Series 2.0 - Node Brass

Manufacturer: Ravenbit
Year: 2014, 2015
Denomination: BTC
Type: UF, DIY

Version	Mintage
DIY LE Serial.	50
DIY Std. No Serial "R"	950
UF Gray Label	150
UF Green Label	30
UF Yellow Label	18
UF Red Label	12
UF Orange Label	6
TOTAL	**1,216**

Material: Brass
Diameter: 39 mm
Thickness: 3 mm
Weight: 26.7 g
Country: USA

1,000 of these brass coins are DIY, the first 50 of which have serial numbers on the back. The other 950 have a stamped 'R' on the reverse.

An additional 216 coins are fully assembled, but not pre-funded. When offered for sale, they sold out in under 10 hours. They have 'A' stamped on the reverse. They come in 'labels' of five different colors which are made in various quantities, with 'label' actually referring to the color of the paper on which the first-bits are written and is visible prominently in the hologram window. These colors are associated with a number of *'s below the first-bits (to ensure that each color can be identified even if faded by the sun or in case of color-blindness; 0 for gray, 1 for green, 2 for yellow, etc).The DIY coin has a different hologram (pictured) than the 'labeled' coins (pictured on the 'Series 2.3 - Node Bronze' page). The purpose of this significant amount of intentional differentiation is to keep collectors interested, as some customers will want to order one of each or most varieties.

Image Credits (clockwise): Elias Ahonen, Ravenbit

Ravenbit

Series 2.1 - Node Copper

Manuf.	Ravenbit
Year	2014
Denom.	BTC
Type	DIY
Mintage	Copper
Material	250
Diameter	39 mm
Thickness	3 mm
Weight	28.8 g
Country	USA

This 'Node' design symbolizes the Bitcoin network and the various 'nodes' that keep it functioning. Just like on the coin, Bitcoin nodes are interconnected so that the network will not be significantly affected even if several dozen nodes are deactivated. The design features 'nodes' in three sizes. The center of the coin features the traditional 'B' in a simplistic setting, notably with no text on that side of the coin. The words 'Bitcoin' and '2014' are on the outer edges of the back. The coin is minimalistic yet highly symbolic, making it attractive to many collectors. These are serialized DIY coins.

Image Credits (clockwise): Howard Kesselman (all)

Ravenbit

Series 2.2 - Node Silver

Manuf.	Ravenbit
Year	2014
Denom.	BTC
Type	DIY
Mintage	.999 Silver
Material	25
Diameter	39 mm
Thickness	3 mm
Weight	1 ozt
Country	USA

This coin has a mintage of only 25 which is extremely low for a .999 silver round or coin, putting its rarity on par with Crypto Imperator's 100,000 DOGE coin. Unlike the copper version which is numbered 01-250, this round has no serial numbers. It is the first silver coin produced by Ravenbit.

Image Credits (clockwise): Howard Kesselman (all)

Ravenbit

Series 2.3 - Node Bronze

Manufacturer: Ravenbit
Year: 2014
Denomination: BTC
Type: UF

Version	Mintage
Gray Label	430
Green Label	27
Yellow Label	18
Violet Label	15
Blue Label	12
Red Label	9
Orange Label	6
TOTAL	**517**

Material: Coated Brass
Diameter: 39 mm
Thickness: 3 mm
Weight: 26.7 g
Country: USA

These 'Antique Bronze' coins are very similar to the Cryptolator '0.1 BTC Antique Bronze Coin, 2014' in finish. They use the same design as the other 'Node' coins, though the antique finish is generally seen as a much higher quality than brass. The same 'color label' system is used, though there are two additional colors (violet and blue) when compared to the brass version. Interestingly, this coin made an appearance on the music video *Ch-Ching* by the Brooklyn-based synthpop band Chairlift in which one of the singers extracts the coin from his mouth.

Image Credits (clockwise): Howard Kesselman (all)

Ravenbit

Series 2.3.1 - Node Bronze 'AT' (Artificially Toned)

Manufacturer: Ravenbit
Year: 2015
Denomination: BTC
Type: UF

Version	First-bits
Mercury	1N6kzAiN
Venus	1N1L4VS7
Mars	1JYc4d23
Jupiter	1Ak4f8MH
Saturn	1NkK3Pmd
Uranus	12HZswGu
Neptune	1H8NdmiJ
TOTAL	7

Material: Bronze
Diameter: 39 mm
Thickness: 3 mm
Weight: 26.7 g
Country: USA

Image Credits (clockwise): Ravenbit (all)

These 'AT' (Artificially Toned) coins are a result of testing undertaken by Ravenbit. These chemical tests destroyed the patina of the bronze, leaving interesting metallic colors on the coins. Though it would be normal to dispose of such coins, Ravenbit demonstrated obvious creativity in naming them after planets (this idea was presumably derived from the colors caused by the chemicals, reminding the viewer of planets). Each of these coins is entirely unique and comes with a standard 'Gray label' hologram.

Above: (Clockwise from top left) Mars, Mercury, Jupiter, Antique Copper (normal), Saturn, and Venus.

Recalescence COINS

Recalescence Coins

Recalescence Coins are created by Dustin Freeman of Australia. Though he intended to produce yearly releases, he only produced one variant. Of this variant, a very small (though unknown) number received a gold plating on the front side only. Dustin's original plan was to sell pre-funded coins, but after Casascius began facing problems with US authorities (FinCEN), Recalescence Coins also began selling on a 'DIY' basis only, with buyers needing to create their own hologram stickers. As such, any coin with a Recalescence hologram is fully funded. Interestingly, each funded coin comes with a certificate containing the public key and an identical hologram (with the same serial number as on the coin).

An interesting thing happened with Recalescence's first customer. Upon finding out that they did not receive the coin with a serial number of 01 though they were the first buyer, the customer accused Dustin of 'fraud' and allegedly blackmailed him demanding the 01 coin in addition to 10 BTC for 'disaster mitigation services' (that is, mitigating disaster by not making public fraud accusations). Dustin refused, and published the text of the email with commentary. Dustin had simply kept the first few coins for himself, family members, and other close supporters. Keeping of the first coins in a series is normal practice for many, if not most manufacturers, and in no way constitutes fraud.

Below: A Recalescence coin being redeemed (left), and the gold 'silverback' version (right)

Image Credits (clockwise):Recalescence Coins, Howard Kesselman

Recalescence

1000mBTC Silver Sparrow

Manuf.	Recalescence Coins
Year	2013
Denom.	1 BTC
Type	PF, DIY
Mintage	500*
Material	.999 Silver
Diameter	39 mm
Thickness	3 mm
Weight	1 ozt
Country	USA

This coin features a bird being set free from its cage, a symbolism creator Dustin Freeman emphasizes when he writes:

"Bitcoin is the idea that freedom should be as unwavering and absolute as the math it is built on. Despite what calamity may befall, or what laws be passed, the protocol is resolute and shall not yield to depredations, fear, or uncertainty".[1]

The coin features a 'chain' with 'blocks' on both ends, symbolizing the blockchain on which Bitcoin is based. Two years are recorded: 2009 to designate the year Bitcoin was launched and 2013 to signify the year of the coin's mintage. The coin is denominated as 1,000 mBTC, the first coin to use mBTC as a standard unit.

* Though a total of 500 were minted, under 200 received holograms and about 300 were sold as blanks. Many coins which were deemed unfit for sale were destroyed (and subsequently melted down) by Dustin.

Though the vast majority of coins are silver on both sides, a small number was gold plated on the front to create variety (and attract more orders). These are known as 'silver backs' and are very rare.

Image Credits (clockwise): Howard Kesselman (2), Unknown

1. Dustin Freeman, source unavailable

SerpCoin

"So I've had a bag of these [Casascius Aluminum Blanks] for a while now and have been working on scripts to create labels along with finding proper labels for them. I have made 48 of them (1 sheet of labels) and funded them with 0.01 bitcoins each. I'm calling this first set version 0.1...I would like to sell around 45 of them for 0.025 btc each plus actual shipping."[1]

In June 2013, perhaps the first coins to imitate Casascius' vision went on sale. Announced four days before Lealana coins, the first small batch of coins made by Bitcointalk.org user 'Serp' can accurately be described as the first raindrop in the coming storm of dozens of coin makers. Perhaps fittingly for being the transition between Casascius and other independent crypto mints, Serp did not mint his own coins but instead used 'aluminum blanks' minted by Casascius and sold with a blank reverse and no hologram.

Serp created two more small batches of funded coins, after which he minted his own line of 'DIY' physical Bitcoins which had a blank reverse and a few custom designed holograms.

It is safe to assume that Serp's initial foray into creating physical Bitcoins was not motivated by profit, but curiosity and a desire to create. He invested his time and energy in a project in which others were interested. This approach is something to keep in mind when examining many of the coins in this Encyclopedia; many are more about expression than business.

Image Credits: SerpCoin

1. "Aluminum Casascius Coins [sold out]" *Bitcoin Talk* 23 June 2013. Link: https://bitcointalk.org/index.php?topic=240768.0

SerpCoin

v0.1

Manuf.	SerpCoin
Year	2013
Denom.	0.01 BTC
Type	PF
Mintage	48
Material	Aluminum
Diameter	31.8 mm
Thickness	1.6 mm
Weight	2.8 g
Country	USA

Created by forum user 'Serp', these coins were made using an ink-jet printer to inscribe the coins before attaching a hologram sticker onto the Casascius 'aluminum round' coins. Serp did exactly what Casascius had envisioned when he used his blank rounds to create his own physical Bitcoin wallets. These coins are significant because they mark the first time that Bitcoin blanks produced by one entity were used by another individual to make and successfully sell pre-funded coins. The 'v0.1' batch was a pilot test for the later SerpCoin releases. It is also notable that this coin is the first containing a serial number; a practice which has since become standard.

Image Credits (clockwise): SerpCoin (all)

SerpCoin

v1, v2

Manufacturer: SerpCoin
Year: 2013
Denomination: 0.05 BTC
Type: PF

Version	Mintage
v1	48
v2	48
TOTAL	**96**

Material: Aluminum
Diameter: 31.8 mm
Thickness: 1.6 mm
Weight: 2.8 g
Country: USA

The 'v1' and 'v2' coins were released after the initial 'v0.1' test batch. This coin uses a slightly higher denomination of fifty millibitcoins, which is the equivalent of 0.05 BTC.

Worth mentioning is that the v0.1, v1, and v2 coins are the first to coins to contain no numeric private key, with a QR code instead being utilized. This has served as inspiration for both bhCoin and Titan Bitcoins. Another notable factor is that these coins often have `first-bits`of only five or 6 characters, instead of the traditional eight.

Image Credits (clockwise): Elias Ahonen, Howard Kesselman

SerpCoin

DIY1

Manuf.	SerpCoin
Year	2014
Denom.	0.25 BTC
Type	DIY
Mintage	500
Material	Zinc Alloy
Diameter	35 mm
Thickness	2.5 mm
Weight	11.9 g
Country	USA

After the successful sale of his initial three batches of coins, Serp produced a new coin of his own design. These coins were sold only in a 'DIY' format, with the blank coin and SerpCoin hologram stickers being shipped together. This coin is not pre-funded with any digital currency, but buyers can obviously do so on their own.

Designated as a 'Quarter Bitcoin', it is the first time the amount of BTC has been represented as a fraction on a physical coin.

Image Credits (clockwise): bitcointalk.org user 'Mitchell', Howard Kesselman

SerpCoin

DIY2

Manuf.	SerpCoin
Year	2014
Denom.	0.25 BTC
Type	DIY
Mintage	1,000
Material	Gold Pl. Zinc Alloy
Diameter	35 mm
Thickness	2.5 mm
Weight	11.9 g
Country	USA

Once the first batch of DIY rounds was sold, SerpCoin released a new round with the same design. This round is plated in 18K gold, and unlike the DIY1 round has a 'Private Key Pit' on the back to better accommodate a private key as shown on the bottom right.

Image Credits (clockwise): Elias Ahonen (2), SerpCoin

SHAcoin

Copper Round

Manuf.	SHAcoin
Year	2014
Denom.	SHA
Type	Round
Mintage	1,500
Material	Copper
Diameter	25 mm
Thickness	1.5 mm
Weight	6 g
Country	Germany

Image Credits: Elias Ahonen

These small copper coins were made to serve as a promotional item for SHACoin, an alternative crypto-currency. Due to the fact that they were made cheaply by using small amounts of metal and the same design on both sides, they were sold very cheaply for only 0.002 BTC each. The design is simple, with the SHACoin logo taking up the center. The rim is simply 'SHACoin' mirrored on both sides, with stars in between which are a common addition to coins when space needs to be filled or something needs to go between different words or statements.

Shibanu

2015 Physical Dogecoin

Manufacturer: Shibanu
Year: 2015
Denomination: 50,000 DOGE
Type: DIY

Version	Mintage
Prototype	100
Regular	500
TOTAL	**600**

Material: Gold Pl. Zinc alloy
Diameter: 38 mm
Thickness: 2.5 mm
Weight: 13 g
Country: UK

Shibanu is based in the UK, and have created a physical Dogecoin as their name might suggest. The coin face is inspired by the Casascius brass coins, and much of the format has been kept the same as a result. The Dogecoin 'D' has a 'doge' peering from behind it in a playful, fun twist that is fitting with the theme.

500 'regular' coins were minted, as well as 100 'prototypes' that were not originally intended for release. They were however serialized and offered as bonuses with each order of five coins or more. The 'prototype' coins have a lower quality finish and a somewhat different design. They also have square private-key pit as opposed to a circular one. A 'prototype' is pictured on the lower right.

Image Credits (clockwise): Howard Kesselman (2), Shibanu (2)

SHIBE MINT

Shibe Mint

Shibe Mint was founded by Tony Pepperoni of Waterloo, Ontario, Canada after he learned all he could about crypto-currency in December 2013. After seeing Casascius coins and learning about the Dogecoin community, he saw an opportunity. In early 2014 he launched the first physical Dogecoin, a 1 oz copper coin. Shibe Mint coins do not include a hologram or contain any DOGE, which was explained by Mr. Pepperoni as an effort to avoid any trouble with money transfer laws. Each coin sold by Shibe Mint does however, come with a 'free gift' paper wallet containing the amount of DOGE stated on the coin.

'Shibe' in the name refers to the Shiba Inu dog breed which is the basis of the 'doge' meme upon which the Dogecoin crypto-currency is themed.

'Very Much Wow', a Dogecoin magazine perhaps offers the best explanation to the uninitiated:

"It's a mind-bender. The wallet is a symbol, is a way for us to accept the idea that we own pieces of something that only exist because we choose to give a bit of nothing value....We believe in Doge, we love Doge, we wish Doge [to be] real, and Doge becomes alive [and gains value] in response."[1]

Image Credits: Shibe Mint

1. "An Interview with Tony of The Shibe Mint" Link: http://www.verymuchwow.com/wp-content/uploads/2014/04/ShibeMintInterview.pdf

Shibe Mint

2014 Pure Copper Ed. (Letter D)

Manuf.	Shibe Mint
Year	2014
Denom.	1 DOGE
Type	Round
Mintage	
Material	Copper
Diameter	39 mm
Thickness	2.6 mm
Weight	1 oz
Country	Canada

This is the first metal round to be created for Dogecoin. Among its main features is a large 'D' for Dogecoin, in contrast with the 'B' which is often seen on Bitcoin rounds and coins. The 'heads' side has the image of a dog, accurately copied from the original meme image which is on the right for comparison. These coins sold for $10 each, and were popular with Dogecoin users who appreciated a low-cost 'physical Dogecoin' similar to what already existed for Bitcoin. It is denominated as '1 Dogecoin'. Several thousand have been sold.

Image Credits (clockwise): Elias Ahonen, Unknown, Elias Ahonen

Shibe Mint

2014 Pure Silver Ed.

Manuf.	Shibe Mint
Year	2014
Denom.	100 DOGE
Type	Round
Mintage	2,500
Material	.999 Silver
Diameter	39 mm
Thickness	2.6 mm
Weight	1 oz
Country	Canada

The production and release of this silver round was risky, due to the very high production costs coupled with such a new and unpredictable target market. Indeed at the time that the minting process was started, it was impossible to know if Dogecoin would even be a 'thing' by the time the rounds were ready. The round design is the same as the original copper round, except its 'D' side is marked for silver content and weight along with a '100 Dogecoins' denomination. It was sold for $35.

Image Credits (clockwise): Elias Ahonen (all)

Shibe Mint

2014 24kt Gold Plated Copper Ed.

Manuf.	Shibe Mint
Year	2014
Denom.	10 DOGE
Type	Round
Mintage	2,500
Material	Gold Plated Copper
Diameter	39 mm
Thickness	2.6 mm
Weight	1 oz
Country	Canada

The gold plated round was created so that a complete range of copper, silver, and gold Dogecoins would be available. A 1oz solid gold version was considered, but it was not likely that there would be many buyers interested when taking into consideration the premium (about 50% of the gold value) that would be required to profitably sell the rounds. Like the other rounds, the outer rim of the 'face' contains words associated with the Dogecoin meme including "Much Coin | Such Money | So Crypto | Plz Mine". It is denominated as '10 Dogecoins' and was sold for $16.99.

Image Credits (clockwise): Shibe Mint (all)

Shibe Mint

Dogecar Commemorative Ed.

Manuf.	Shibe Mint
Year	2014
Denom.	98 DOGE
Type	Round
Mintage	1,098
Material	Copper
Diameter	39 mm
Thickness	2.6 mm
Weight	1 oz
Country	Canada

This copper round commemorates the 'Dogecar' which is among the more momentous achievements of the Dogecoin community to date. In March 2014, Dogecoin users on the website Reddit raised 67 million Dogecoin ($55,000) to sponsor NASCAR driver Josh Wise for the 2014 'Aaron's 499' race. The race was held on May 4th, 2014 at the Talladega Superspeedway in Alabama, where Wise finished 20th in car #98 which was wrapped in a massive advertisement for Dogecoin. The car was nicknamed the 'Moon Rocket' as a nod to Dogecoin users' common saying that Dogecoin would soon go "to the moon" (massively increase in value), and perhaps even as a tongue-in-cheek expectation that the publicity garnered by the sponsorship would indeed 'rocket' the value of Dogecoin 'to the moon'. Josh Wise himself developed a liking for the Dogecoin community, and continued his partnership with them by rallying users to vote for him in fan-favorite contests and even released a Dogecoin t-shirt to finance further races. In reference to the car number, this round is denominated as '98 Dogecoins' and was even listed as having an original price of $98, though it was on perpetual 'sale' for $10.

Image Credits (clockwise): Shibe Mint, Elias Ahonen

Silver Shield Collection

Paradigm Failure

Manuf.	Silver Shield Collection
Year	2014
Denom.	BTC / Various
Type	Round
Mintage	
Material	.999 Silver
Diameter	39.3 mm
Thickness	3 mm
Weight	1 ozt
Country	USA

This round is made by Silver Shield Collection, a company that makes a large number of silver bullion coins and bars. Most of the material created by Silver Shield is based around Libertarian themes. Their designs promote sayings like 'Don't tread on me', the right to bear arms, and mock the US federal monetary system. The criticism aimed at the established financial system is often done with the implication that precious metals such as silver are 'real' money as opposed to government issued money.

What makes this Bitcoin themed round truly special is that it is not actually meant to promote Bitcoin in any form. The 'BitCON' round is meant to mock the idea of Bitcoin and crypto-currencies, with the implication that they are intangible and therefore worthless (or at least without intrinsic 'real' value) just like dollars, euros, and pounds apparently are. The round has a large Bitcoin 'B' symbol (which is technically incorrect, as it only has one vertical stroke), inside of which smaller dollar, euro, and pound signs are found. 'Paradigm Failure' is superimposed in the center, and the outer rim of the round states 'You Don't Own It If You Don't Hold It'. The divergence in opinions on crypto-currency is most interesting.

Image Credits (clockwise): Elias Ahonen (all)

SILVERWALLETS.com

Silver Wallets

The USA based Silver Wallets was launched in March 2014, and is owned by four individuals named Adam Graham, Alex Dearth, Doug, and Keeth. The idea behind the company is to create high quality DIY (self assembled) Bitcoin wallet rounds and bars. The team behind the company is highly professional: both Adam and Doug individually have good reputations as resellers and traders of physical crypto-currencies, whereas Alex is a rare coin dealer in Washington DC.

Quite notably, Adam (unsuccessfully) offered his 23.5% ownership stake in the company for sale in January 2015 (and again in June of that year). The listing offered a revealing glimpse into the inner workings of a 'crypto-mint'. Adam calculated the 'total retail value' of the company's assets to be $34,600, of which he offered 23.5% for a 'starting bid' of $7,000. These assets included $25,000 in stock at retail value in addition to 4,000 holograms, three dies for the coins ($3,100 value), and a die for the Silver Wallets hologram ($2,500 value). It was also advertised that the debt-free company has the names and contact information of all 350+ customers, an established reputation, and that "the remaining partners have a desire to diversify into bars, gold coins, base metal wallets, and accessories".[1]

Many observations can be made from this listing, the most striking of which is perhaps the stated cost of the dies needed to make the coins and holograms. Since the die to mint a coin can cost in excess of $1,000, it is a significant barrier of entry and means that small mintage lots must carry a significantly higher cost. For example, the cost of the die would only need to account for $1 per coin in a 1,000 coin series (such as Silver Wallets' first round), but $40 per coin in a limited mintage of only 25 such as Crypto Imperator's 100,000 DOGE coin. Another thing to take into account is the stated cost of the hologram die, which was used to create the holograms and is needed if the same hologram is to be printed in a larger quantity. Though many manufacturers have used more than one hologram design, it is important to realize the cost that changing the design entails.

Since the company has only sold fine silver rounds that are particularly well made (perhaps in part because one of the owners is a rare coin dealer), it has gained a very good reputation as being a producer of high quality, luxury coins.

Image Credits: Silver Wallets

1. " Silver Wallets Business" *Bitcoin Talk* 5 February 2015. Link: https://bitcointa.lk/threads/silver-wallets-business.418636/

Silver Wallets

Design 1

Manufacturer: Silver Wallets
Year: 2014
Denomination: BTC
Type: DIY

Version	Mintage
Serial	100
Non Serial	200
TOTAL	**300**

Material: .999 Silver
Diameter: 39 mm
Thickness: 3 mm
Weight: 1 ozt
Country: USA

This is the first round produced by Silver Wallets, and can be seen as the 'flagship' product due to its mintage number and the gold variation. It features the 'B' symbol with a backdrop of the world map, with binary code covering up the empty space taken up by oceans. The text above states 'Universale Monetae' which is Latin for 'universal money'. The backside prominently features the Silver Wallets name, along with the engraved serial number (001-100) of the first 100 of coins.

Image Credits (clockwise): Elias Ahonen, Silver Wallets

Silver Wallets

Design 2

Manuf.	Silver Wallets
Year	2014
Denom.	BTC
Type	DIY
Mintage	100
Material	.999 Silver
Diameter	39 mm
Thickness	3 mm
Weight	1 ozt
Country	USA

The centrally placed 'B' in this round is surrounded by several currency symbols, suggesting that Bitcoin is superior to the dollar, euro, and yen, as well as silver and gold. The round prominently features a complex mathematical equation; a first for physical crypto-currencies. The equation is taken from the Bitcoin white paper by Satoshi Nakamoto which laid the foundations for Bitcoin. A '51% attack' is a legitimate concern for Bitcoin, as it is technically possible for someone who controls 51% or more of the total mining power to essentially 'hijack' the blockchain and manipulate it.

Image Credits (clockwise): Elias Ahonen (all)

Silver Wallets

Design 1 with Gold Trim

Manuf.	Silver Wallets
Year	2014
Denom.	BTC
Type	DIY
Mintage	100
Material	.999 Silver
Diameter	39 mm
Thickness	3 mm
Weight	1 ozt
Country	USA

This round is made with the same mold as the first silver round, but has a 24 karat gold plating on the sides and 'B'. All 100 are serialized 001-100.

Image Credits (clockwise): Howard Kesselman (all)

Silver Wallets

Design 3

Manuf.	Silver Wallets
Year	2015
Denom.	BTC
Type	DIY
Mintage	100
Material	.999 Silver
Diameter	39 mm
Thickness	3 mm
Weight	1 ozt
Country	USA

This round has a similar profile as the other gold-plated round, but is simpler in design. It does not feature any interesting designs, nor convey deep symbolism or messages. It is simply to be used as a 'silver wallet' that conveys the value of the BTC it is holding. The plating is 24 karat gold and each round is serialized 001-100.

Image Credits (clockwise): Howard Kesselman, Silver Wallets

Socal

1 oz .999 Fine Silver Physical Vericoin

Manuf.	Socal
Year	2014
Denom.	VRC
Type	PF
Mintage	100
Material	.999 Silver
Diameter	39 mm
Thickness	3 mm
Weight	1 ozt
Country	USA

This coin was produced by Socal, a user of the Bitcointalk forum who did not use any separate business name for this coin production initiative. The coin is designed to hold Vericoin, which is an alternative crypto-currency (and part of 'Supernet' for which another physical coin exists). Seven of the coins were set aside for the Vericoin's developers, and 55 were given to pre-announcement donors to the project. The remaining 38 coins were sold for 0.1 BTC each, with half due at reservation and the other half due prior to shipping which took place about five months after the announcement.

The front features the Vericoin 'V' logo and the Latin phrase 'Ad Infinitum – 2014' which translates to 'To Infinity – 2014'. The backside has a hologram and the text 'First Edition'.

Image Credits (clockwise): Howard Kesselman (all)

Sol Noctis

Binary Eagle

Manuf.	Sol Noctis
Year	2014
Denom.	0.01 BTC
Type	PF
Mintage	2,009
Material	.999 Silver
Diameter	39 mm
Thickness	3 mm
Weight	1 ozt
Country	Poland

This coin stands out amongst physical Bitcoins in design and execution. They are distributed by TopWorldCoins, a major seller of custom low-mintage collectible coins. The fact that such a large company is interested in being the sole distributor of a pre-funded physical Bitcoin gives the format a legitimacy that cannot be easily attained by the efforts of small independent producers who do not have visibility to the wider coin-collecting market. The coin was "created to mark the point where two worlds meet: traditional numismatics and a payment system of the future, and so to push the limits of both of them".[1]

The front is taken up by the face of an eagle, whose feathers are composed of 1's and 0's in a nod to binary code which has become a common theme in physical crypto-currency since the very beginning. The eagle represents the unrestricted freedom that Bitcoin provides its users. The back hologram is very unique because it is not circular and takes up only a small portion of the backside. The hologram displays the Earth with other planets, which morphs into the Bitcoin symbol when the coin is rotated.

Image Credits (clockwise): Howard Kesselman (2), Sol Noctis (1)

Supernet

1st Edition Supernet Coin (Silver)

Manuf.	Supernet
Year	2015
Denom.	Various - N/A
Type	Round
Mintage	350
Material	.999 Silver
Diameter	39 mm
Thickness	3 mm
Weight	1 ozt
Country	USA

Supernet is an 'association' or teamwork initiative by the developers of several alternative crypto-currencies to share ideas, and technologies. Several 'alt coins' are part of the association, with seven of them being featured on this round. These are (clockwise from top on the front) Opal, VPNcoin, Boolberry, BitcoinDark, Chancecoin, VeriCoin, and NXT. The Center of the coin features a large 'U', which stands for 'Unity' and is made to resemble a stereotypical crypto-currency symbol. Though the backside seems like it could accommodate a hologram, it is not meant to do so.

Image Credits (clockwise): bitcointalk.org user 'minerjones' (all)

Supernet

1st Edition Supernet Coin (Antique Silver)

Manuf.	Supernet
Year	2015
Denom.	Various - N/A
Type	Round
Mintage	35
Material	.999 Silver
Diameter	39 mm
Thickness	3 mm
Weight	1 ozt
Country	USA

On the backside below the Supernet logo, are the words 'Unite – Reward – Share', signifying the foreseen positive outcomes of the Supernet initiative. The creator of the coins believes that Supernet is the future of crypto-currencies. They have anticipated that once the association is successful in combining its talents to create a truly ground-breaking crypto-currency, the rounds will have significant historical value.

1st Edition Supernet Coin (Gold Pl.)

Manuf.	Supernet
Year	2015
Denom.	Various - N/A
Type	Round
Mintage	35
Material	Gold Pl. .999 Silver
Diameter	39 mm
Thickness	3 mm
Weight	1 ozt
Country	USA

The silver coins originally sold for 50 USD, while the Antique silver coins went for 80 USD. The gold plated coins were priced the highest, at 100 USD per coin. As an effective marketing tactic, they were sold on various crypto-currency forums and appealed to both users and developers of each featured currency.

Image Credits (clockwise): Supernet (2), nxtforum.org user 'rubenaco' (2)

TGBEX

A part of what makes TGBEX special is its location in the Isle of Man, which has been very permissive towards bitcoin. TGBEX (The Global Bitcoin EXchange) is operated by Adrian Forbes, who is an accountant and investment advisor with 15 years of experience. The coins launched in September 2014, when a prototype was put for sale on eBay and sold for 265 GBP.

TGBEX is run in a highly professional manner, with a very active and informative website and Twitter page. Mr. Forbes has appeared on BBC radio and has garnered interest from mainstream UK news outlets for his coins. Especially impressive about the company is the ambitiousness of creating large-denomination physical bitcoins in 2 BTC, 5 BTC, 10 BTC, 20 BTC, and even 50 BTC (with 1 BTC being valued at approximately $500 at the time of launch). With coins as valuable as these, it is clear that TGBEX is aiming for a much different market than its competition; one which Mr. Forbes certainly understands via his profession. Unlike most crypto-mints, TGBEX has been in active talks with various regulatory bodies and is working towards being the first fully regulated maker of physical Bitcoins.

Instead of having a printed private key like the 'normal' physical bitcoins, TGBEX engraves the complete private key on the back of each coin. This is certainly a premium touch, similar to what is done by Alitin Mint.

A maximum mintage limit has been set for each coin (999 each for brass-alloy coins and 499 for each of the silver coins), but at the time of writing that number has not actually been produced for any coin. Each of the silver coins is hallmarked by the Birmingham assay office, for yet another layer of authenticity and class.

Image Credits: TGBEX

TGBEX

One Bitcoin

Manuf.	TGBEX
Year	2014
Denom.	1 BTC
Type	PF
Mintage	499
Material	Silver Pl. Brass
Diameter	43 mm
Thickness	3 mm
Weight	34.7 g
Country	Isle of Man

The TGBEX coins look the same overall, but have different finishes and denominations. They read 'The Global bitcoin Exchange' on the outer front, while the middle features a complete world map in a 'sea' of Bitcoin 'B' symbols. Each coin is serialized. The range is truly remarkable, from 0.5 BTC to 50 BTC. The back hologram features a similar world map, and is the same for each coin.

Image Credits (clockwise): TGBEX, Howard Kesselman

TGBEX

Half Bitcoin

Manuf.	TGBEX
Year	2014
Denom.	0.5 BTC
Type	PF
Mintage	499
Material	Ant. Brass
Diameter	43 mm
Thickness	3 mm
Weight	34.7 g
Country	Isle of Man

Two Bitcoin

Manuf.	TGBEX
Year	2014
Denom.	2 BTC
Type	PF
Mintage	499
Material	Gold Pl.
Diameter	43 mm
Thickness	3 mm
Weight	34.7 g
Country	Isle of Man

Five Bitcoin

Manuf.	TGBEX
Year	2014
Denom.	5 BTC
Type	PF
Mintage	499
Material	Ant. Gold Pl.
Diameter	43 mm
Thickness	3 mm
Weight	34.7 g
Country	Isle of Man

Image Credits (clockwise): TGBEX (all)

TGBEX

Ten Bitcoin

Manuf.	TGBEX
Year	2014
Denom.	10 BTC
Type	PF
Mintage	99
Material	.999 Silver
Diameter	43 mm
Thickness	3 mm
Weight	
Country	Isle of Man

Twenty Bitcoin

Manuf.	TGBEX
Year	2015
Denom.	20 BTC
Type	PF
Mintage	99
Material	.999 Silver
Diameter	43 mm
Thickness	3 mm
Weight	
Country	Isle of Man

Fifty Bitcoin

Manuf.	TGBEX
Year	2015
Denom.	50 BTC
Type	PF
Mintage	
Material	.999 Silver
Diameter	43 mm
Thickness	3 mm
Weight	
Country	Isle of Man

Image Credits (clockwise): TGBEX (all)

Titan Bitcoin

Titan is based in California, launched in October 2013, and is led by Tim Fillmore. When launched, the entire offering of six coins was announced right away, instead of adding designs as the previous ones sold out. This is evidence of a larger up-front investment and risk taken by the company. Titan Bitcoin (also known as Titan Mint) was the second mint to produce a 1 oz gold Bitcoin, after Casascius. It is notable that in just over two years, the BTC denomination for a 1 oz gold coin went from 1,000 BTC to 1 BTC; evidence of the immense growth in BTC value in a short period. Titan originally expressed an intent to produce 5 BTC and 10 BTC coins in silver and gold (at which time one bitcoin was worth about $200). Two months later (when BTC had doubled to $400), the 1 BTC denomination gold coin was announced.

The coins made by Titan Bitcoin introduced a new and unique design aspect in their holograms. They expanded Casascius' design of using a hologram 'window' to verify the coin's contents by adding a much larger window and a QR code by which anyone could quickly check and verify the amount of BTC confined inside the coin. A Coin ID number is also printed beneath the QR code. Unlike some coin manufacturers, Titan Bitcoin has succeeded in projecting a highly professional image with a well-designed website and online ordering mechanism.

Titan Bitcoin guarantees the balances of its coins by 110 percent "if ANY customer of ours ever loses money because of a security breach in our system."[1] Replicas of Titan Bitcoin's coins have been mass-produced in China, with identical imagery on the front but a very different back. They have not been 'malicious' in the sense of a fraudulent hologram; the backsides simply feature an alternate design consisting of a QR code in the metal in the spot where the hologram would normally be placed.

Image Credits: Titan Bitcoin

1. "Titan Bitcoin Security" Link: https://www.titanbtc.com/titan-bitcoin-security/

Titan Bitcoin

Titan One

Manuf.	Titan Bitcoin
Year	2013
Denom.	1 BTC
Type	PF
Mintage	10,000*
Material	Goldine**
Diameter	34 mm
Thickness	2 mm
Weight	12 g
Country	USA

*Maximum mintage. Real production numbers unknown.

** Cupro-nickel alloy 230

These coins by Titan are either normal 'wallet' type coins or 2-factor storage coins. The actual production and circulation numbers are unknown, though there is a 10,000 limit.

Image Credits (clockwise): Howard Kesselman (all)

Titan Bitcoin

Titan One - 1oz Silver

Manuf.	Titan Bitcoin
Year	2013
Denom.	1 BTC
Type	PF
Mintage	1,000
Material	.999 Silver
Diameter	39 mm
Thickness	3.3 mm
Weight	1 ozt
Country	USA

The face of the coin depicts a Greco-Roman hero, preparing for war. This hero is a personification of the bitcoin community. "With eyes gazing confidently forward, the hero prepares for the battle as digital currency fights for acceptance on the global economic stage. To the right of the hero, is the Latin motto of 'Unum Pecuniae' which roughly translated means, 'One currency for all'".[1] Following the Ancient Greek theme, the hologram side features a Laurel Wreath on the lower rim. 'One Troy Ounce | .999 Fine Silver' is written into the inner rim.

Image Credits (clockwise): Howard Kesselman (all)

1. "Titan One - 1oz Silver" Link: https://www.titanbtc.com/product/titan-one-silver/

Titan Bitcoin

Titan One - 1oz Gold

Manuf.	Titan Bitcoin
Year	2014
Denom.	1 BTC
Type	PF
Mintage	1,000*
Material	.999 Gold
Diameter	34 mm
Thickness	
Weight	1 ozt
Country	USA

*Maximum mintage. Real production number is likely 200 or less

Produced in batches of 100, this is by far the largest mintage for a solid gold physical crypto-coin. For comparison, Casascius minted only a few 1 oz gold coins, and Crypto Imperator minted 10 half ounce coins.

This coin is a testament to the significant amount of funding behind Titan Bitcoin, with each batch costing well in excess of 120,000 USD to produce. Few manufacturers have even reached total sales in excess of that amount.

Image Credits (clockwise): Titan Bitcoin (all)

Titan Bitcoin

Titan Half

Manuf.	Titan Bitcoin
Year	2014
Denom.	0.5 BTC
Type	PF
Mintage	10,000*
Material	Goldine
Diameter	34 mm
Thickness	2 mm
Weight	12 g
Country	USA

*Maximum mintage. Real production numbers unknown.

In addition to first-bits, the hologram features a QR code visible through the window. Though there is an announced limit of 10,000 coins, the actual production and circulation numbers are not known. When the hologram is peeled, it leaves a 'VOID VOID VOID' pattern making it clear that the coin is not secure.

As with the 'Titan One', 'Unum Pecuniae' is inscribed on the face, which is Latin for 'One currency for all'.

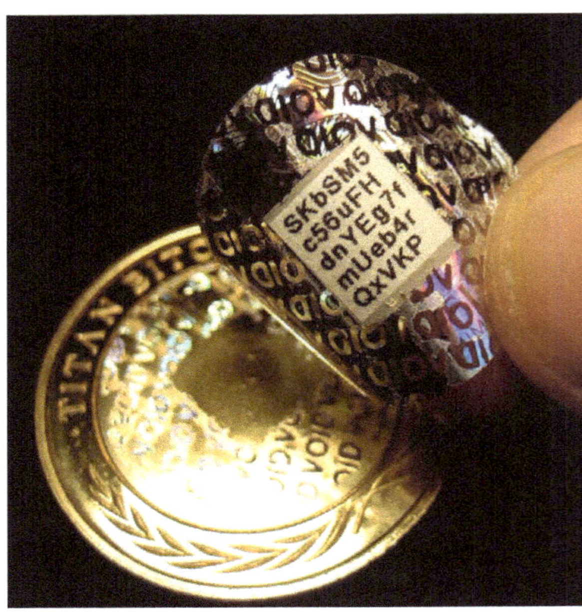

Image Credits (clockwise): Howard Kesselman, Titan Bitcoin

Titan Bitcoin

Titan Half - 1oz Silver

Manuf.	Titan Bitcoin
Year	2014
Denom.	0.5 BTC
Type	PF
Mintage	2,500*
Material	.999 Silver
Diameter	39 mm
Thickness	3.3 mm
Weight	1 ozt
Country	USA

*Maximum mintage. Real production numbers unknown.

The face of the coin depicts a "historical symbol of power, the Lion is a personification of... bitcoin itself. Boldly unafraid of confronting the threats that loom in front of it, the lion deeply embodies the spirit of bitcoin."[1]

In promotional material, Titan uses a famous quote by St. Augustine: "The truth is like a lion. You don't have to defend it. Let it loose and it will defend itself." Though St. Augustine was certainly not referring to a digital currency's apparent superiority, the meaning translates well.

Image Credits (clockwise): Howard Kesselman (all)

1. "Titan Half – 1oz Silver" Link: https://www.titanbtc.com/product/titan-half-silver/

Titan Bitcoin

Titan Tenth

Manuf.	Titan Bitcoin
Year	2014
Denom.	0.1 BTC
Type	PF
Mintage	10,000*
Material	Nickel-Silver Alloy
Diameter	31.8 mm
Thickness	
Weight	12 g
Country	USA

*Maximum mintage. Real production numbers unknown.

The product description for this coin covers the desired points of explanation and analysis:

"The face of the coin depicts the Roman god, Mercury. As the swift messenger of mythology, Mercury was called upon to deliver vital messages with unmatched speed. Symbolically, Mercury has also historically been associated with freedom of thought. With eyes gazing upward towards his destination, this coin depicts Mercury taking flight as a representation of the speed and freedom that bitcoin represents."[1]

Image Credits (clockwise): Howard Kesselman (all)

1. "Titan Tenth" Link: https://www.titanbtc.com/product/titan-tenth/